BLACK LABOR
IN AMERICA,
1865–1983

BLACK LABOR IN AMERICA, 1865–1983

A Selected Annotated Bibliography

Compiled and edited by JOSEPH WILSON

with the assistance of THOMAS WEISSINGER

Bibliographies and Indexes in Afro-American and African Studies, Number 11

Greenwood Press
New York • Westport, Connecticut • London

Library of Congress Cataloging-in-Publication Data

Wilson, Joseph, 1951-
  Black labor in America, 1965-1983.

  (Bibliographies and indexes in Afro-American and
African studies, ISSN 0742-6925 ; no. 11)
    Includes index.
    1. Afro-Americans—Employment—Bibliography.
I. Weissinger, Thomas. II. Title. III. Series.
Z7164.L1W54   1986   016.3316'3'96073   86-349
[HD8081.A65]
ISBN 0-313-25267-X (lib. bdg. : alk. paper)

Library of Congress Catalog Card Number: 86-349
ISBN: 0-313-25267-X
ISSN: 0742-6925

First published in 1986

Greenwood Press, Inc.
88 Post Road West, Westport, Connecticut 06881

Printed in the United States of America

The paper used in this book complies with the
Permanent Paper Standard issued by the National
Information Standards Organization (Z39.48-1984).

10 9 8 7 6 5 4 3 2 1

CONTENTS

INTRODUCTION

The history of the Afro-American people is a mosaic woven into the fabric of the history of labor in America. This objective fact has stimulated into existence a wide range of literature on the subject. While the literature on Black labor is large, it is widely scattered and often difficult and time consuming to access. Many writers, particularly at the doctoral thesis level, have expressed frustration at the the process of accessing relevant literature on Black workers. Accessibility, however, is secondary, to the problem and limited analysis of exclusion of Black labor from American labor literature in general.

The existing literature on Black labor reveals only the tip of deeply rooted involvement in social upsurges, including the Civil Rights Movement, the Women's Movement, the New Deal, populism and unionization, (especially CIO organizing drives during the 1930's and 1940's) in which Black workers played an important role. Numerous titles relevant to these movements have been included in this text.

Black labor leaders and rank and file trade unionists initiated, and were the organizational core of the Civil Rights Movement. This social upsurge of the oppressed gained national attention in 1941 as the March on Washington Movement (MOW), led by A. Philip Randolph of the Brotherhood of Sleeping Car Porters, forced President Franklin D. Roosevelt to create the Fair Employment Practices Committee.

Between the 1940's and 1960's in every city and town, north and south, that developed a viable local civil rights organization, Black workers were participating in and/or leading the struggle. For example, Rayfield Mooty, founder of the Black Caucus Movement in the United Steelworkers of America[1], and Vice President of the Chicago Negro Labor Council, was a civil rights activist as well. Folowing the brutal 1950's murder of Emmett Till, Mooty insisted that Till's body, grotesque from torture, be viewed by the public, and this created a massive civil rights event in Chicago.

In the South, as a precursor to the 1960's Civil Rights struggles, Dr. Martin Luther King became involved in leading the Montgomery Bus Boycott and the Southern Christian Leadership Conference based on the encouragement from the leaders of the Brotherhood of Sleeping Car Porters.[2]

Hillard Ellis, Afro-American President of the huge, influential United Auto Workers (UAW), Local 457 in Illinois, fought to desegregate

public facilities in Chicago, Detroit, and in Sears and Roebuck
department stores. Ellis and his local were among the earliest union
financial supporters of Dr. King before he was nationally known.[3]
    Cleveland Robinson, Secretary Treasurer of District 65,
Distributive Workers, was a leading organizer of the 1963 and 1983
Marches on Washington, was on the Board of Directors of the Southern
Christian Leadership Conference, and was one of Dr. King's most trusted
labor allies who provided resources, people, and thousands of dollars in
membership contributions from the union for the struggle.[4]
    In 1967, William Lucy, Secretary Treasurer of the million (plus)
member American Federal State County and Municipal Employees (AFSCME),
acted as the union negotiator during the Memphis Sanitation Workers
strike.[5]
    Dr. King's involvement in the sanitation Worker's struggle for human
dignity was not simply a politically expedient gesture of reciprocity
towards labor for their firm, longstanding support. Rather, King's
active support of the Sanitation Workers symbolized his recognition of
the fundamental role played by workers, especially the most down
trodden, in the Civil Rights Revolution. Dr. King's assasination in
Memphis, occurred while he was fighting for his union brethren, and
represented the ultimate sacrifice one can make for a cause. The
national civil rights marches on Washington in 1963 and the twentieth
anniversary in March 1983[6] were organized and mobilized by Black labor
and called for Black-White unity to overcome discrimination. Hundreds
of lesser known marches in those decades were often organized and
mobilized by Black labor working within the Black church. Little has
been written about the momentous relationship between the Labor and
Civil Rights Movements. Most of the literature overlooks, or
underestimates the role played by Black workers as catalysts for social
change both as leaders and foot soldiers of a mass movement.
    This bibliography was in part stimulated as a result of the
exclusion of Black labor in a quantitative and qualitative sense from
the dominant mainstream literature, including bibliographic literature
on Black labor. Examples of exclusion, omission or underanalysis of the
role of the Black worker in the American political economy are abundant.
    Problems exist with current reference publications in relation to
Afro-American labor. The G.K. Hall Publishing Company has reproduced
the card catalogs of some of the major Afro-American history
collections, for example, the Schomburg Center for Research in Black
Culture, the Arthur B. Spingarn Collection of Negro Authors, the Negro
Collection of the Fisk University Library, the Vivian G. Harsh
Collection of Afro-American History and Literature, and the Jesse R.
Moorland Collection of Negro Life and History. To access a small
portion of the literature on Black labor, one must spend considerable
time looking through the thirty or more volumes comprising G.K. Hall's
book catalogs. Still, this would not afford anything approaching a
comprehensive coverage of the literature in this field.
    There is a great deal of literature on Black labor which is not
included in the G.K. book catalogs, nor is it included in other
bibliographies identifying books in the broader field of Afro-American
history. Not included are manuscripts in special collections, museums
and individual private buildings. In addition, there are manuscript
collections, for example, the A. Philip Randolph Institute in New York
which is neither accessible through the standard bibliographies nor
available physically at other research libraries.
    To further complicate Afro-American research, book catalogs and

bibliographies which include books on Black labor in the United States
differ significantly in the application of subject headings and
descriptors. There are approximately sixty Library of Congress subject
headings which are used to organize literature about Blacks and labor.
About one half of these are derived from the eighth edition subject
headings. Use of "Negro", "Negroes" and "Negroes in" still provide
subject control of books cataloged using the eighth edition subject
headings. These terms and phrases give way to "Black", "Blacks", and
"Afro-American" in the ninth edition of the Library of Congress subject
headings. Also, there are more subtle differences, e.g., current use of
the phrase "Afro-American air pilots" as opposed to "Negroes in
aeronautics"; or "Afro-American motion picture actors and actresses" as
opposed to "Negroes in the motion picture industry". Necessarily,
diverse subject headings bury the corpus of literature on Black labor.
Thus existing literature becomes diffused, obscure and often
inaccessible.

Moreover, individual libraries modify Library of Congress subject
headings for their own purposes and further complicate subject control
of books on Black labor. For example, in the book catalog of the Vivian
G. Harsh Collection, the subject of Blacks and labor unions receive the
heading "Labor Unions and the Negro laborer". In the Jesse E. Moorland
Collection book catalog the same subject receives the subject heading
"Trade Unions". The book catalog for the Schomburg Center used the
subject heading "Labor Unions and the Negro". The literature retrieval
system is so complicated for Black labor that even many people skilled
in the library sciences are unaware of the subtleties of research in
this area. Although this bibliography does not address the problem of
accessing scattered manuscript collections, it does assemble a large
number of monographs and applies systematic subject categories.

It is a logical irony, given the dominating influence of racism,
elitism, and class oppression in the intellectual and real history of
America, that the vast majority of literaure on Black workers is
generated neither by Blacks, workers, nor even scholars who necessarily
held the interest of Black workers at heart. Indeed, some studies
appeared to have been intended to justify, or more firmly and
efficiently fasten the rod of exploitation to the Black worker. The
literature on Black labor, in its entirety, attests to the inherent
character of employment discrimination in virtually every sector and
time period to the present of the American political economy. Studies
of cities, towns, regions, and occupations in relation to the racial
distribution of employment opportunity since the Civil War, almost
universally reveal structural discrimination against Black workers in
every sphere of economic existence, and with significant social
consequences for poverty, health, education, housing, and politics. The
condition of Black America is based fundamentally on the condition of
labor.

This bibliography is an attempt to survey the diverse field of
Afro-American labor literature after the Civil War. Approximately one
thousand texts that were considered for inclusion, 583 appear here, over
90% of which have been annotated. Much of the material in this
bibliography was cross-indexed, and categorized according to what
appeared to be its central focus and approach to the study of Black
labor. The literature was also categorized into convenient groupings
for researchers, such as women and wages.

Given the size, scope and historical range of this project, no
attempt is made to be comprehensive in every category, occupation or

discipline. In some areas, this volume is a cross sectional survey, rather than an exhaustive one. However, books available from commercial publishers and dissertations are identified on a scale as comprehensive as possible given the resources available at Rutgers University. Theses were surveyed when available and included selectively.

Books, pamphlets, government documents, dissertations predominantly about Black labor were included; whereas literature more concerned with Black economic development, urban relations, poverty studies, or labor in general, without specific focus on Black workers, were not included. Books primarily about Black labor before the Civil War were not included, as there are numerous excellent bibliographies of Afro-American slavery. The abolitionist movement in America, although having labor as a central issue, is also the subject of numerous bibliographies, and is therefore not the focus of this bibliography.

Over one hundred privately funded or sponsored studies of black labor have been included-- with the Ford Foundation the single most important resource of philanthropic assistance. Other private studies of Black labor were either unavailable for review, or too narrow in focus for this bibliography.

Journal articles on Black labor were not included unless published separately in pamphlet form. However, a good number of the published titles on Black labor include collections of articles and papers appearing separately in journals.

In some cases biographies and autobiographies were included, insofar as extensive light was shed on the occupational status of Black labor. However, employment and occupational categories were excluded from this study, for example, professional athletes, the military, musicians and certain other cultural workers. Neither religious nor political employment fell within the parameters of this study. Studies of illegal labor (the underground economy) and prison labor were also excluded.

Many of the important governmental studies have been included. However, given the multi-layered and overlapping governmental processes, some governmental studies may have been overlooked. Some agencies and divisions of government generating data on Black workers includes the legislative, executive and judicial arms operating at the federal, state and local levels.

As a whole, the literature paints a portrait of decades of generational exploitation and generations of resistance to oppression. A myriad of forms and levels of discrimination in the division of labor are treated in relation to what is simultaneously a specific and general process of racial bifurcation in the workplace.

Black workers have been the subject of studies by historians, economists, anthropolgists, sociologists, political scientists, labor scholars, corporations, philanthropic organizations, journalists, lawyers, psychologists, the government, unions, and various Afro-American organizations. This volume draws from the interdisciplinary method in representing diverse methodological and philosophical approaches to the topic of Black labor.

It is hoped that this volume will help facilitate the study of Black labor in order to ameliorate an oppressed status which has endured far too long. The end of employment discrimination in America, however, is not yet in sight.

All mistakes, shortcomings, and ommissions are my own. Constructive criticism is welcome. I wish to express my appreciation to all those who helped me in this endeavor. My special thanks go to Tom Weissinger, an outstanding librarian and Afro-American bibliographic specialist.

Without his invaluable assistance, this project would have been extremely difficult to complete. Thanks also to Peg Law for processing hundreds of interlibrary loans.

A number of organizations within Rutgers University are to be thanked for extending to me their financial and moral suppport, including the Research Council; the Department of Africana Studies; the Minority Faculty Development Committee; and the library system.

My gratitude is also extended to Peggy Gilchrest who deciphered and typed my notes, Shawn Donaldson for her meticulous typing of the final draft, and to my wife Maria for typing, filing and supplying boundless encouragement needed to complete this project. This manuscript is dedicated to my father, Charles Wilson, who put me on the right path in life.

FOOTNOTES

[1]Rayfield Mooty, personal interview (Chicago: 1977). Professor Miriam Balanoff of Roosevelt University in Chicago is preparing a detailed history of Mooty.

[2]Joseph Wilson, Documentary Video Interview of Benjamin McLaurin. Sponsored by the Schomburg Center for Research on Black Culture. Producer, James Murry. Transcribed by Columbia University, Department of Oral History.

[3]Joesph Wilson, Personal Interview of Hillard Ellis. Chicago: 1981. Transcribed by Columbia University, Department of Oral History.

[4]Joseph Wilson, Documentary Video Interview of Cleveland Robinson. personal taped interview, 1982. Columbia University Department of Oral History, 1983.

[5]Joesph Wilson, Documentary Video Interview of William Lucy, Washington, D.C., Columbia University, Schomburg Library, 1983.

[6]A. Philip Randolph was a principle sponsor of the 1963 March on Washington. In 1983, thousands of Black and white trade unionists, many from AFSCME, turned out for the Civil Rights Anniversary March. In 1963, the AFL-CIO voted not to endorse the march. However in 1983, the March was endorsed by the AFL-CIO Executive Council.

[7]This encompasses congressional hearings and studies, legislation, especially Title VII of the 1964 Civil Rights Act, executive orders, employment guidelines, and studies: thousands of cases of litigation and consent decrees: Studies by the Departments of Labor; Health, Education and Welfare; the Civil Rights Commission, Freedmans Bureau (Reconstruction); and the WPA Program of the 1930's (Works Progress Administration); state reports, programs, policies and agencies in relation to Black labor, (particularly discrimination), as well as city, county and congressional district reports.

BIBLIOGRAPHY

Beard, Charles and Mary, <u>The Rise of American Civilization</u>.   New York:
    McMillian, 1933.
Beard, Mary, <u>The American Labor Movement</u>. New York: MacMillian, 1931.
<u>Bibliographic Guide to Black Studies</u>. Boston: G.K. Hall, 1976. Annual
    Volumes.
<u>Dictionary Catalog of the Jessie E. Moorland Collection of   Negro Life
    and History</u>. Vols. I-IX. Boston: G.K. Hall, 1970.
<u>Dictionary Catalog of the Negro Collection of the Fisk University
    Library</u>. Vols. I-VI. Boston: G.K. Hall, 1974.
<u>Dictionary Catalog of the Schomberg Collection of Negro Literature and
    History</u>. Vols. I-IX. Boston: G.K. Hall, 1962.
_____. First Supplement. Vols. I,II.
    Boston: G.K. Hall, 1967.
_____. Second Supplement. Vols. I-IV.
    Boston: G.K. Hall, 1972.
_____. Supplement 1974. Boston:
G.K. Hall, 1976.
Dubofsky, Melvyn, <u>When Workers Organize</u>. Amherst: University of
    Massachusetts Press, 1969.
Shostac, Arther, <u>Blue Collar Life</u>. New York: Random House, 1969.
<u>The Chicago Afro-American Union Analytic Catalog: An Index to Materials
    on the Afro-American in the Principle Libraries of Chicago</u>. Vols.
    I-V. Boston: G.K. Hall, 1972.

BLACK LABOR
IN AMERICA,
1865–1983

ANNOTATED
BIBLIOGRAPHY

1.   Adedeji, Moses. "Crossing the Colorline: Three Decades of the
United Packinghouse Workers of the America's Crusade Against Racism in
the Trans-Mississippi West, 1936-1968". Diss. North Texas State, 1978.

   The story of the Packinghouse Workers from the birth of the
   union to the Civil Rights period.

2.   Alabama. Advisory Committee to the U.S. Commission on Civil
Rights. Where are Women and Blacks?. Washington, D.C.: GPO, 1979.

   A discussion of patterns of Black and female employment in
   Alabama State Government.

3.   Albrier, Frances. Frances Albrier. Interview. Cambridge:
Radcliffe College/Black Woman Oral History Project,   n.d.

   Frances Albrier of Berkeley, California, a social worker
   and political community leader for 35 years, was
   instrumental in eliminating discrimination in the hiring of
   teachers in the Berkeley schools.

4.   Alexander, James. Blue Coats: Black Skin. New York: Exposition
Press, n.d.

   A brief outline history of Black police in New York City
   from 1891 to 1977.

5.   Alexander, Richard D. et al. The Management of Racial Integration
in Business; Special Report to Management. New York: McGraw-Hill, 1964.

6.   Alex, Nicholas. Black in Blue. New York: Appleton-Century-
Crofts, 1969.

   This book is about some of the conflicts and contradictions

faced by Black New York City Police officers assigned to a
variety of duties in 1964-65. Indepth interviews were
conducted with 41 officers to form the basis of the
research data.

7.   Alston, Christophere. Henry Ford and the Negro People. New York:
Schomburg Collection, n.d.

A look at the relationship between the founder of the Ford
Motor Company and Blacks, especially in Detroit.

8.   American Academy of Political and Social Science. The Industrial
Condition of the Negro in the North.   Publication No. 498.
Philadelphia: 1906.

9.   American Negro Labor Congress. The American Negro Labor Congress
Constitution. New York: Schomburg Collection, n.d.

This document was adopted at the Congress' first national
convention held in Chicago (1925).

10.   Anderson, Bernard. The Opportunities Industrialization Centers: A
Decade of Community-based Manpower Services. Racial Policies of American
Industry, Report No. 6 . Philadelphia: Wharton School/Industrial
Research Unit, 1976.

A detailed look at the OIC- A Black community-based self
help organization. Also included in this series:

Educating the Employed Disadvantaged for Upgrading (1972)
          -Richard Rowan & Herbert Northrup
Manpower in Homebuilding (1974)
          -Howard Foster
The Impact of Government Manpower Programs (Encyclopedic
analysis, 1979)
          -Charles Perry
          -Bernard Anderson, et al.
Manpower and Merger (1976)
          -Steven S. Plice

11.   Anderson, Bernard E. Energy Policy and Black Employment: A
Preliminary Analysis. Racial Policies of American Industry.
Philadelphia: Wharton School/Industrial Research Unit, 1978.

A limited discussion of the relationship between a national
energy policy and Black employment prospects. Industrial
labor force trends are viewed with a prescriptive
(educational) analysis.

12.   Anderson, Bernard E. The Negro in the Public Utility Industries.

Philadelphia: Wharton School/Industrial Research Unit, 1970. (See
Northrup, Negro Employment in Basic Industry).

13.   Anderson, Jervis. A. Philip Randolph: A Biographical Portrait.
New York: Harcourt Brace Jovanovich, 1970.

    A sympathetic detailed discussion of the struggles and
    victories of the leader of the Brotherhood of Sleeping Car
    Porters, in connection with his historical circumstances.

14.   Anthony, Carl. Blacks in Construction. Berkeley: University of
California, 1977.

    An historical look at Blacks in construction and
    architecture from African times to modern construction
    industry. Contributors include William Gould, Herbert
    Northrup and Booker T. Washington.

15.   Arata, Esther Spring. Black American Playwrights 1800 to Present:
A Bibliography. Metuchen: Scarecrow Press, 1976.

    A listing of 190 Black American playwrights along with
    their specific literary contributions.

16.   Arata, Esther Spring. More Black American Playwrights: A
Bibliography. Metuchen: Scarecrow Press, 1978.

    A more detailed listing of the accomplishments of Black
    playwrights, and an extension of the author's earlier work
    on the subject.

17.   Ashburn, Elizabeth Alexander. "Influences and Motivations for
Black and White Women to Attain Positions in a Male-dominated
Profession".   Diss. State University of New York at Buffalo, 1979.

    An examination of personality and situational variables of
    28 Black and 32 white female doctorates employed in
    universities.
    The study substantiated the theoretical expectations of the
    author insofar as achievement patterns were found to be
    formulated during childhood and career patterns resulted
    from social conditions. Among various comparisons Black
    women viewed their achievement level as circumstantial,
    whereas whites viewed their achievement level as based on
    childhood experiences.

18.   Ashenfelter, Orley and Heckman, James. Measuring the Effect of an
Anti-discrimination Program. Princeton: Princeton/Industrial Relations
Section, 1974.

The authors utilize Equal Employment Opportunity data to
statistically chart anti-discriminatory efforts relating to
federal contract compliance.

19.   Bailer, Lloyd. "Negro Labor in the Automobile Industry".   Diss.
University of Michigan, 1943.

A study undertaken between 1939-1942 of Black auto workers
in relation to management, white labor and organized labor.

20.   Baker, Henry Edwin. The Colored Inventor. New York: Arno Press,
1969.

A brief discussion of notable Black inventors who lack
social recognition.

21.   Bancroft Library. Pacific Coast Division Records. Sleeping Car
Porters. Berkeley: n.d.

One of the best collections of documentary material
relative to the west coast Brotherhood.

22.   Banks, Eugene. "Career Aspirations of Black Male Principals in
Large North Eastern Ohio Cities".   Masters thesis University of Akron,
1974.

A comparison of the career aspirations of 177 white and 33
Black male principals in Ohio cities.

23.   Barnum, Darold T. The Negro in the Bituminous Coal Mining
Industry. Philadelphia: Wharton School/Industrial Research Unit, 1970.
(See Northrup, Negro Employment in Basic Industry).

24.   Barone, Sam. The Impact of Recent Developments in Civil Rights on
Employers and Unions. Chicago: Commerce Clearing House, 1966.

The author looks at the 1964 Civil Rights Act in relation
to integration in unions and industry.

25.   Baron, Harold M. The Demand for Black Labor. Somerville: New
England Free Press, 1971.

This pamphlet briefly explores the transformation of
Black slave labor to Black industrial labor in the context
of a mature capitalist society. Exploitation, racial
conflict, labor segregation and demographic tendencies in
metropolitan centers are viewed from the perspective of
(Marxist) political economy.

26.   Baron, Harold M. and Hymer, Bennett. <u>Negro Workers in the Chicago</u>
<u>Labor Market</u>.   Chicago: Chicago Urban League, 1968.

       This study examines the central elements in Chicago's
       defacto labor segregation.

27.   Becker, Gary S. <u>The Economics of Discrimination</u>.   Chicago:
University of Chicago, 1957.

       An economic and statistical look at the forces of
       discrimination active in the market economy.   The author
       argues that discrimination reduces incomes of employers and
       employees.   The human capital theory forms the basis of his
       hypothesis.

28.   Bennetts, David Paul.   "Black and White Workers: New Orleans,
1880-1900".   Diss. University of Illinois, 1972.

       Focusing on New Orleans, this study is concerned with race
       relations between Black and white workers (on and off the
       job), Jim Crow, the Knights of Labor, the AFL and Booker T.
       Washington during the 1880-1900 period of social conflict
       and economic recession.

29.   Bergman, Barbara. <u>Curing High Unemployment Rates Among Blacks and</u>
<u>Women</u>.   Springfield: N.T.I.S., 1972.

       The author argues for changes in labor market dynamics
       which would place Blacks and women in the same favored
       economic status traditionally only enjoyed by white males,
       by utilizing quotas.

30.   Blood, Robert O. Jr. <u>Northern Breakthrough</u>.   Belmont: Wadsworth,
1968.

       A case study of fair employment in Minneapolis and St. Paul
       retail stores.

31.   Bloom, Gordon F. and Fletcher, F. Marion. <u>The Negro in the</u>
<u>Supermarket Industry</u>.   Philadelphia: Wharton School/Industrial Research
Unit, 1972.   (See Northrup, <u>Negro Employment in Basic Industry</u>).

32.   Blumrosen, Alfred. <u>Black Employment and the Law</u>.   New Brunswick:
Rutgers University Press, 1971.

       An important legal and scholarly approach to the issues of
       job discrimination, seniority, the EEOC, the Civil Rights
       Act and federal employment policy.

8   Annotated Bibliography

33.   Bobo, Benjamin F. and Osbourne Jr., eds. Emerging Issues in Black Economic Development. Lexington: Lexington Books, 1976.

A business, financial and consumer oriented study of Black economic development.

34.   Bolden, Richard L. "A Study of the Black Guardian Organization in the New York City Police Department from 1943-1978". Diss. Columbia, 1980.

A look at the formation, policy and practice of the Black caucus movement inside the N.Y.P.D.

35.   Borelli, Albert J. "The Sales Management - Production Management Social Dychotomy: Occupational Assimilation of Negro Employees and Other Implications". Diss. University of Pittsburgh, 1971.

This study focuses on the resistance of Black occupational assimilation in sales management positions, within the context of the dichotomy of sales and production management, and utilizing a survey questionaire given to management, executive recruiters and business school deans.

36.   Bouch, Richard F. "Perceptions of Supervisory Techniques by Black and White Teachers and Principals in Selected Florida Schools". Diss. University of Florida, 1976.

An opinion survey of 150 Black and white teachers and supervisors concerning their perception of supervisory techniques.

37.   Bowen, William A. and Finegan, T. Aldrich. The Economics of Labor Force Participants. Princeton: Princeton University, 1969.

A scholarly overview of the dynamics of labor force participation delineated into useful categories including race, gender, age, etc. Surprising data are presented that often contradicts the dominant literature in regards to Blacks and women.

38.   Bracy, John et al. Black Workers and Organized Labor. Belmont: Wadsworth, 1971.

A collection of notable articles discussing discrimination in the ranks of organized labor.

39.   Bramwell, Jonathan. Courage in Crisis. Indianapolis:

Bobbs-Merrill, 1972.

A non-scholarly, personal view of Black professionalism.

40.   Brazeal, Brailford R. The Brotherhood of Sleeping Car Porters.
New York: Harper & Brothers, 1946.

One of the best and most detailed studies of the
Brotherhood, covering the employment status of Black
Pullmen porters, the birth and development of the
Brotherhood, the relations between the community and the
Brotherhood, contract negotiations, structure and function
of the Brotherhood, legal conflicts, the AFL-CIO, wages,
etc.

41.   Brisbane, Robert H. The Black Vanguard: Origins of the Negro
Social Revolution, 1900-1960. Valley Forge: Judson Press, 1970.

A detailed survey of employment campaigns during the
Depression.

42.   Brookings Institution. Jobs and Civil Rights. U.S. Commission on
Civil Rights. Washington, D.C.: GPO, 1969.

One of the best and most detailed discussions of Title VII
of the 1964 Civil Rights Act and Executive Order 11246
(covering employers with government contracts, and federal
employment services relating to equal opportunity).
The EEOC, created by Title VII, is the centerpiece of labor
related civil rights legislation. A useful bibliography is
contained at the conclusion.

43.   Brookins, Geraldine K. "Maternal Employment: It's Impact on the
Sex Roles and Occupational Choices of Middle and Working Class Black
Children".   Diss. Harvard, 1977.

A study of the occupational choices made by Black children
whose mothers work, and exert psychological job orientation
on their off spring.

44.   Brooks, Barbara Jean Roberts. "A Profile of Black Females in
Selected Administrative Positions in the Public School Systems in
Florida".   Diss. University of Michigan, 1975.

This descriptive study is concerned with collecting
biographical and statistical data on Black female school
administrators in Florida. In order to present a profile
of sex and racial status of the above, a
survey-questionaire method is employed.

45.   Broome, Homer F. Jr. LAPD's Black History, 1886-1976.
[S.L.]: Stockton Trade Press, 1977.

A detailed look at the Los Angeles Police Department's
employment of Black officers.

46.   Brown, Charles. Black/White Earning Ratios Since the Civil Rights
Act of 1964: The Importance of Labor Market Drop-outs. Cambridge:
National Bureau of Economic Research, 1981.

47.   Brown, Earl and Leighton, George. The Negro and the War. New
York: AMS Press, 1942.

A brief look at Black employment and discrimination in the
United States Armed Forces. Union and federal racial
employment policies are also examined.

48.   Brown, Morgan C. "Evaluation of Jobs and Occupations by Negroes
of Columbus, Ohio". Diss. Ohio State, 1955.

A localized urban analysis of industrial employment trends
of post WWII Black workers in Columbus.

49.   Brown, Myland Rudolph. "The IWW and the Negro Worker".   Diss.
Ball State, 1968.

A detailed analysis and positive assessment of Black-white
relations in the Wobblies-International Workers of the
World (IWW). The author contends that the IWW removed
racial barriers especially in Louisiana, Texas, Norfolk,
Philadelphia and Baltimore.

50.   Brown, Pat A. "Racial and Professional Identities".   Diss.
University of Chicago, 1971.

A study of the relationship between Black social workers,
the Associations of Black Social Workers, and the
integrated National Association of Social Workers. A
survey method was used to determine perceptions and
behavioral differences amongst the groups.

51.   Brown, Ronald Richard. "Coping Strategies Used by Black
Professionals".   Diss. University of Michigan, 1977.

A look at how Black professionals cope with and respond to
a discriminatory status, limited upward mobility and
professional.

52.   Brunn, Paul D. "Black Workers and Social Movement of the 1930's

in St. Louis".   Diss. Washington, 1979.

A descriptive, highly detailed case study of racism and the
exploitation of Black labor, trade unionism, and working
class social movements in St. Louis - with special focus on
radical organizations, the trade union unity league, The
American communist party, and the CIO.

53.   Bullock, Paul. Aspirations v. Opportunity: "Careers" in the Inner
City. Ann Arbor: University of Michigan, 1973.

An optimistic and reformist analysis of Black and Chicano
youth employment.

54.   Bullock, Paul. Merit Employment: Nondiscrimination in Industry.
Los Angeles: University of California/Institute of Industrial Relations,
1960.

A scholarly discussion of employment discrimination and how
to combat it.

55.   Bunte, Frederick. "An Inquiry into the Decline in the Number of
Blacks Entering the Teaching Profession".   Diss. Ohio State, 1972.

An attempt to explain the recent (pre-1972) decline of
Blacks entering the teaching profession. Class values,
racial barriers and greater non-educated job opportunities
are discussed as causal factors.

56.   Bureau of National Affairs Incorporated. State Fair Employment
Laws and their Administration. Washington, D.C.: 1964.

A detailed look at anti-discrimination laws in 22 states.

57.   Burt, Walter Lee. "The Impact of the 1964 Civil Rights Act -
Title VI and Title VII - On Employment of Black Administrators in
Michigan School District from 1964-1974".   Diss. University of
Michigan, 1975.

This study attempts to determine the extent and and impact
of Affirmative Action programs in advancing Black school
administrators in Michigan.

58.   Butler, Carol A. "An In-depth Investigation of the Vocational
Development Patterns of Fourty Black American Professional Men from Lower
Socio-economic Level Families".   Diss. New York, 1970.

A study of 40 Black New York men, utilizing interview data,
which includes in a non-generalizable fashion, that these
individuals had family life styles more closely resembling

middle class, rather than lower class families. Their life
styles, the author contends, is unrelated to their
professional accomplishments.

59.   Butler, Richard John. "Black/White Wage and Employment Changes: A
Look at Production Workers in South Carolina 1940-1971".   Diss.
University of Chicago, 1979.

A look at education, industrial trends, and supply and
demand determinants concerning Black workers in South
Carolina between 1940-1971.

60.   California. Division of Fair Employment. Negroes and Mexican
Americans in South and East Los Angeles. Los Angeles: the Division,
1966.

An analysis of population, employment, income and family
status of Blacks and Latinos in Los Angeles between 1960
and 1965.

61.   California. State Personnel Board. The Status of Black Employees
in the California State Civil Service. Sacramento: the Board, 1977.

A description of the 1977 employment status of Blacks in
California's State Civil Service.

62.   Carpenter, Niles. Nationality, Color and Economic Opportunity in
the City of Buffalo. Buffalo: University of Buffalo/Roswell Park
Publication Fund, 1927.

63.   Cator, Milton. Black Labor in America. Westport: Negro
Universities Press, 1969.

An outstanding collection of useful essays focusing on
diverse post-Civil War and pre-WWII social and economic
conditions of Black labor in specific regions and
nationally.

64.   Cavanagh, Gerald Francis. "Black and White Workers' Attitudes in
Three Industrial Plants: View From the Grassroots".   Diss. Michigan
State, 1970.

A look at employment conditions and race relations in three
electrical factories, attempting to convey the thinking of
300 workers, management, and unionists based on interviews
reflecting a divergence of opinions. The study is
generally optimistic at the employment progress made by
Blacks, yet recognizes the existence of racial barriers.

65.   Cayton, Horace R. and Mitchell, George S. Black Workers and the New Unions. 1939; rpt. Chapel Hill: University of North Carolina Press, 1969.

Recognized as a classic in the field of Black labor literature, the authors present a detailed description and analysis of Black labor during a period of upsurge in industrial unionism. The steel, meat packing and railroad industries between 1910-1930 are given special attention. An excellent bibliography is presented on labor up to 1934.

66.   Center for the Studies in Vocational and Technical Education. The Education and Training of Racial Minorities, Proceedings of a Conference May 11-12, 1967. Madison: University of Wisconsin, 1968.

This study reflects the author's optimism of the early 1960's-the ability to solve minority underemployment through skills development. The participants included Walter Fogel, James Farmer, Louis Ferman and Lester C. Thurow.

67.   Chalmers, Ellison and McCormick, Gerald. Racial Conflict and Negotiation. Detroit: University of Michigan/Wayne State, 1971.

A Ford Foundation sponsored study of the 1968 Memphis sanitation workers strike and Black water employees in Cleveland.

68.   Chambers, Rita C. "An Identification and Comparison of Problems Encountered by Black and Women Superintendents".   Diss. University of Iowa, 1979.

A survey of Black/female public school superintendents with respect to problems related to race and gender.

69.   Chicago Historical Society. Manuscript Division. Brotherhood of Sleeping Car Porters. Chicago: n.d.

This Brotherhood collection has a local and regional focus.

70.   Christian, Charles Melvin. "The Impact of Industrial Relocations from the Black Community of Chicago upon Job Opportunities and Residential Mobility of the Central City Work Force".   Diss. University of Illinois, 1979.

An examination of the "suburbanization" process as related to industrial relocation and residential movement in the city of Chicago and the surrounding metropolitan area. Empirical data concerning industrial demographics are used to show trends and historical patterns of development.

71.   Christian, Marcus. <u>Negro Ironworkers of Louisiana, 1718-1900.</u>
Gretna: Pelican Publishers, 1972.

    A brief, scholarly detailed, look at the skills and
conditions of labor experienced by Black ironworkers in
Louisiana, especially New Orleans.

72.   Cincinnati. Chamber of Commerce. <u>The Status of the Negro in</u>
<u>Industry and Occupational Opportunities in Cincinnati.</u> Cincinnati: the
Chamber, 1930.

    An optimistic assessment of Black employment progress in
Cincinnati.

73.   Clark, William R. "The Assimilation of the Negro Teacher in
Massachusetts".   Diss. Colorado State, 1967.

    This study explores the status of Black elementary and
secondary school teachers in Massachusetts. Perceptions
and social relations are probed utilizing a survey method.

74.   Cobb, Nimrod. "In-service Education for Black Teachers of
Vocational Teachers of Vocational Agriculture in Alabama".   Diss. Ohio
State, 1974.

    The purpose of this study was to improve
agricultural/vocational teaching in Black in-service
teachers training programs in Alabama.

75.   Cobb, William L. <u>Motivation of the Black Worker.</u> Springfield:
U.S. Department of Commerce, 1972.

    Theoretical and methodological consideration is given to
expectancy theory literature and organizational psychology
in the context of motivation and the Black worker. A good
psychology bibliography is included.

76.   Coles, Robert. <u>Migrants, Sharecroppers, Mountaineers.</u> Boston:
Little Brown, 1971.

    A multi-disciplinary approach to racial exploitation of
Black and white children.

77.   Coley, Soraya Moore. "And Still I Rise: An Exploratory Study of
Contemporary Black Private Household Workers".   Diss. Bryn Mawr
College, 1981.

    One of the best studies of female Afro-American domestic
workers.

78.   Commission on Professional Rights and Responsibilities. Task
Force Survey of Teacher Displacement in Seventeen States. Washington,
D.C.: National Education Association, 1965.

   An assessment of the impact of school desegregation on
   Black teachers, in an effort to estimate and limit the
   displacement of Black faculty in 11 Southern and 6 border
   states.

79.   Connecticut. Commission on Human Rights. Minority Group
Integration by Labor and Management. Hartford: the Commission, 1953.

   A study of the employment practices of large employers, and
   the membership practices of unions with respect to race,
   national origin, etc.

80.   Conway, Mimi. Rise Gonna Rise. Garden City: Anchor Press, 1979.

   A discussion/portrait of Black and white southern textile
   workers as presented by several contributors/workers.

81.   Cooke, Alfred Wynwood. "A Comparison of Middle-class
College-educated Black Men in Traditional and Nontraditional
Occupations".   Diss. Ohio State, 1974.

   A descriptive study and survey of 81 Black men in relation
   to attitudinal and biographical characteristics, and
   occupational variables. Non-traditional occupational
   choices stem from social dynamics, whereas traditional jobs
   are systematically prepared.

82.   Cornfield, Noreen. "Local Industrial Unions: Political
Competition and Negro Representation".   Diss. University of Chicago,
1971.

83.   Cousens, Francis R. A Study of Patterns of Discrimination in
Employment. Ann Arbor: University of Michigan/Wayne State, 1966.

   This study was conducted by Wayne State University's
   Institute of Labor and Industrial Relations for the Equal
   Employment Opportunity Commission.

84.   Cox, Marcelino. Second Class Suburbanites: White Blue-collar
Suburbs and Black Blue-collar Suburbs. Monticello: Council of Planning
Librarians, 1975.

   A bibliographic series of the class characteristics of
   occupation, education, religion, etc., of suburban Black

and white workers.

85.   Crane, Donald Paul. "Qualifying the Negro for Professional Employment".   Diss. Georgia State, 1970.

An attempt to provide guidelines for minority employment programs relating to Black salaried employees and career development. Fifty-eight Black and white salaried employees and twenty-five personnel officers were interviewed focusing on Atlanta, and revealing specific forms of discrimination against Black salaried workers.

86.   Crawley, Brenda. "Determinants of Labor Force Participation During the Retirement Decade: An Analysis of Aged Black Males and Aged White Males".   Diss. University of Illinois at Champaign-Urbana, 1981.

A descriptive study concerning labor force comparisons of Black and white men during their pre-retirement, ages 60-69. Socio-economic factors stimulating and limiting labor force participation are discussed as the author suggests a greater incentive exists for white males to participate more actively in the retirement decade.

87.   Crigler, William R. "The Employment Status of Blacks in Los Angeles: Ten Years After the Kerner Commission Report".   Diss. Claremont Graduate School, 1979.

A combination of statistical and interview data were used to evaluate the impact of the Kerner Commission Report on unemployment and underemployment. A pessimistic picture is presented concerning the lack of progress made to improve the Black employment situation in Los Angeles.

88.   Cripps, Thomas. Slow Fade to Black: The Negro in American Film, 1900-1942. New York: Oxford University Press, 1977.

A thoughtful presentation of the Black role in American film from 1900-1942.

89.   Crossland, William A. Industrial Conditions Among Negroes in St. Louis 1914. Rochester: University of Rochester, n.d.

An outstanding survey of Negro occupations, wages, working conditions and unionism in the early 20th century in St. Louis. Coupled with interviews, 2832 workers' schedules were used as an empirical base. Employers were also surveyed.

90.   Crosswaith, Frank. Frank Crosswaith Papers. New York: Schomburg Collection, n.d.

Founder and long term chairman of the Negro Labor Committee
(1935), who was active in Harlem politics relating to labor
and union issues. (See Negro Labor Committee)

91.   Crump, William L. "A Study of the Employment Problems of Negro
Office Workers in Integrated Work Programs with Implications for Business
Education".   Diss. Northwestern, 1949.

One of the few studies of Black office employees in
connection with Black-white race relations.

92.   Cull, John G. and Hardy, R.E., eds. Career Guidance for Black
Adolescents: A Guide to Selected Professional Occupations. American
Lectures in Social and Rehabilitation Psychology. Springfield: Charles
C. Thomas, 1975.

93.   Daniels, Virginia. "Attitudes Affecting the Occupational
Affiliation of Negroes".   Diss. University of Pittsburgh, 1938.

This study focuses on the effort to change problems and
attitudes toward the Negro which affects his choice of
vocation and his opportunity to engage in the more socially
desirable occupations.

94.   Datcher, Linda P. "The Effects of Higher Woman's Labor Force
Participation Rates on the Relative Earnings of Black and White
Families".   Diss. Massachusetts Institute of Technology, 1978.

The author describes the effects of female employment
relative to the family income of Blacks and whites, and
empirically examines job competition, vis-a-vis higher
labor participation rates.

95.   Davis, Angela. Women, Race and Class. New York: Random House,
1981.

The author explains, utilizing a classic Marxist approach,
the historic nature of oppression of Black women in America
from slavery to modern times. The differences between
Black and white women's movements are explored from the
anti-slavery period, the sufferage period, 20th century
unionization. Male chauvanism, abortion, and communism are
also discussed. The perspective and arrangement of the
data is unique to the literature on the Black woman who are
a class of workers "in the first place". Davis' synthesis
of Afro-American female radicalism is essential in any
discussion of Black women and labor in America.
Popular, traditional, and non-traditional secondary sources
constitute the bulk of qualitative data used in rendering
an anaysis of Black women in a capitalist and sexist

society. Quantitative data are not employed.

96.   Davis, Howard. Contributions of Blacks to the Physical Education Profession. Birmingham: Alabama Center for Higher Education, 1978.

A survey of the contributions made by Black physical education intructors to that field.

97.   Davis, N.F. "Trade Unions' Practices and the Negro Workers - The Establishment and the Implementation of the AFL-CIO Anti-discriminatory Policy". Diss. Indiana, 1960.

An analysis of the AFL-CIO's anti-discriminatory policy as it affects Blacks participation in unions, with emphasis on the differences between craft and industrial unions.

98.   Daymont, Thomas N. Pay Premiums for Economics Sector and Race: A Decomposition. Columbus: Center for Human Resource Research, 1979.

A brief look at some theoretical considerations pertaining to employment discrimination.

99.   Dellums, C.L. C.L. Dellums, International President of the Brotherhood of Sleeping Car Porters and Civil Rights Leader: An Interview. Berkeley: University of California/Bancroft Library, 1973.

Dellums, one of the key leaders of the Brotherhood, discusses his life and times.

100.   Denby, Charles. Indignant Heart: A Black Workers Journal. Boston: South End Press, 1978.

A series of vignettes revolving around the author's life and politicization process. One of the few books written by a Black worker.

101.   Deskins, Donald Richard Jr. "Residential Mobility of Negro Occupational Groups in Detroit". Diss. University of Michigan, 1971.

102.   Dewing, Rolland Lloyd. "Teacher Organizations and Desegregation, 1954-1964". Diss. Ball State, 1967.

A look at the National Education Association, the American Federation of Teachers in relation to the impact of the Brown v. Board of Education (Topeka) decision.

103.   Dill, Bonnie T.   "Across the Boundaries of Race and Class: An
Exploitation of the Relationship between Work and Family among Black
Female Domestic Workers".   Diss. New York, 1979.

A study presenting the relationship between the employer
and employees as essentially a class relationship with
operative racial factors reinforcing the employees inferior
position. Twenty-six Black American female household
workers age 60 to 81 in New York and Philadelphia were
interviewed for primary data. Details of life, work and
family relationships outline perceptions as well as
objective linkages between domestic work and conditions of
labor.

104.   Dill, Lowell.   "Industrial Pursuits of Employed Negroes in the
Major Industries of Bessemer, Alabama as Related to an Adult Vocational
Training Program".   Diss. University of Colorado, 1936.

This study attempts to develop a program of vocational
training for Negro workers in major industries located in
Bessemer, Alabama.

105.   Douglas, Priscilla.   "Black Working Woman".   Diss. Harvard,
1981.

A case study based on intensive interviews of 23 Black
female blue collar employees on the Harbour Company
(Boston), in relation to the impact of job experiences on
employment opportunity perceptions. Factors influencing
employment are discussed, as are theories of discrimination
and labor market segmentation. The differences between
Black and white female employment experiences are
attributed to race.
Generalizing from the Harbour Company data, the author
demonstrates that Black women move into jobs formerly held
by white women. Black women do not replace white men in
filling employment opportunities. The inadequacy of
opportunity theory is discussed in light of historical race
and sex discrimination.

106.   Douglas, Priscilla H.   "Black Working Women: Factors Affecting
Labor Market Experience".   Paper No. 39.   Wellesley: Wellesley Center for
Research on Women, 1980.

A look at the disadvantages of being a Black woman in a
discriminatory labor market. The author compares Black and
white working women, and reviews the literature offering
explanations for racial/sexual female differences. Useful
bibliography.

107.   Drake, Maylon.   "Employment of Negro Teachers".   Diss.
University of California, 1963.

108.   Dubinsky, Irwin. Discrimination in the Construction Industry:
Operation Dig and Its Legacy. New York: Praeger, 1968.

A case study of a Philadelphia protest organization's
(Operation Dig) efforts to obtain employment equality in
the construction trades. The book is written from the
standpoint that change coming from the top down is better
than change from the bottom up based on social upsurges and
people's movements.

109.   DuBois, W.E.B.   Black Reconstruction in America, 1860-1880.   New
York: Harcourt Brace, 1935.

Recognized by many as the best study on the Reconstruction
period. DuBois offers an outstanding discussion, analysis
and social critique of the status of Black workers in the
post Civil War South. Black workers are discussed in
relation to white workers and property relations. The
Black proletariat in South Carolina, Mississippi and
Louisiana are the focus of special chapters and discussed
in a detailed historic context.

110.   DuBois, W.E.B.   The Negro Artisan. Atlanta: Atlanta University
Publisher, 1902.

A classic study of the barriers faced by Black workers,
especially skilled workers, stemming from racist,
exclusionary policies of labor unions at the turn of the
20th century.

111.   DuBois, W.E.B.   The Philadelphia Negro. 1899; rpt. Series in
Political Public Law No. 14. New York: Benjamin Blum, 1969.

A classic and one of the first (1899) publications in
American urban sociology (Black or white). Dubois inquired
deeply into the daily lives, employment conditions, social
affiliations and oppressed racial status of 4,000 Black
Philadelphians. He develops an intricate survey of their
family life, home life, and living quarters, etc. in a
scientific and personal census type house to house
approach. The subjects of this study were escentially
working class and detailed information about their health,
religious habits, political observations, crime, etc., make
this study both a unique and well rounded scholarly
treatise.
An empirical analysis of Negro domestic service in
Philadelphia's 7th Ward, written by Isabel Eaton, follows
the text, as does a useful bibliography.

112.   Dummett, Clifton.   Afro-American Dentistry.   Los Angeles: Dummett,
1978.

 A chronological survey of Blacks in the field of dentistry
 from 1740 to 1975.

113.   Dutcher, Dean.   "The Negro in Modern Industrial Society: An
Analysis of the Changes in the Occupations of Negro Workers, 1910-1920".
Diss. Columbia, 1931.

 An excellent study of the influx of Black workers into
 emerging 20th century industries. Written and published at
 the same school, and at the same time that Abram Harris
 wrote his famous thesis The Black Worker, Dutcher was
 overshadowed by Harris' work.

114.   Eberhardt, Mae.   Mae Eberhardt.   Interview.   Cambridge: Radcliffe
College/Black Woman Oral History Project, n.d.

 Mae Eberhardt of Newark, New Jersey, became involved in
 union activity as a laundry worker in the 1940s; she served
 as a shop steward for 12 years and was active in
 negotiations and grievances; as an electronics worker, she
 became part of the International Union of Electrical, Radio
 and Machine workers where she was elected local president
 and served as chief negotiator; she has held many other
 union positions.

115.   Edge, Karl A.   "White/Black Differences in Hours of Work Supplied
by Men 45 to 59".   Diss. Ohio State, 1973.

 A highly specific analysis of wage differentials between
 Black and white middle aged workers and an assessment of
 the causal factors creating the statistically verified
 differentials.

116.   Edwards, Gilbert Franklin.   The Negro Professional Class.   Diss.
University of Chicago, 1952.   Westport: Greenwood Press, 1982.

 This monograph is a study of Black professional
 stratification and mobility in the District of Columbia.

117.   Edwards, Marvin.   "A Study of the Employment of Black
Superintendents and Principals in Illinois Public Schools".   Diss.
Northern Illinois, 1974.

 This study surveys the perceptions and opinions of Black
 principals and superintendents (115 total) in Illinois
 (excluding Chicago) vis-a-vis community, staff and
 employment conditions.

118.   Elward, Elizabeth. Constitutional and Statutory Provisions of the States. Vol. XIII. Chicago: The Council of State Governments, 1958.

   The first half of this book is a summary study of State Employment Practices, citing state laws and statutes.

119.   Engerrand, Steven William. "'Now Scratch or Die': The Genesis of Capitalistic Agricultural Labor in Georgia, 1865-1880". Diss. University of Georgia, 1981.

120.   Englander, Frederick Jay. "Economic Variables Affecting the Labor Market Status of Black Women". Diss. Rutgers, 1975.

   The minimum wage, labor market elasticity and business cycle employment hypothesis are examined utilizing single factor regression analysis. The author challenges traditional concepts pertaining to Black and female employment, while recommending wage subsidies as a method to improve wages without increasing unemployment.

121.   Erbe, Brigitte M. "The Redistribution of Black Males in the American Occupational Structure - 1950-1970". Diss. University of Iowa, 1973.

   "An analysis of the changing occupational status of non-white males in the occupational structure of the United States from 1950-1970".

122.   Ervin, J. McFarline. "The Participation of the Negro in the Community Life of Los Angeles". Diss. University of Southern California, 1931.

   A dated and superficial view of pre-1930 Black employment in Los Angeles covering a range of categories from agriculture to prostitution.

123.   Everett, Faye P. The Colored Situation. Boston: Meador, 1936.

   A detailed analysis and collection of essays concerning the problems of vocational training and Negro employment during the 1930's.

124.   Fadayomi, Theophilus. "Black Women in the Labor Force: An Investigation of the Factors Affecting the Labor Force Participation of the Black Women in the United States". Diss. University of Pennsylvania, 1977.

   A study, utilizing census data, of Black female labor participation between 1940-1970, especially financial factors helping or hindering participation.

125.   Feldman, Herman. Racial Factors in American Industry: A Study of
Racial Tensions and Conflicts over the Issue of Black Entry into the
Skilled Craft Trades. New York: Harper Brothers, 1931.

    One of the best presentations of early 20th century
    employment discrimination in the skilled trades.

126.   Ferguson, Elaine. "The Relationship of Work Motivation to
Selected Demographic Characteristics of Black Female Workers".   Diss.
University of Houston, 1976.

    A sample of 258 Black female workers "to determine whether
    a significant relationship exists between Black female
    workers' needs and work values and specific demographic
    characteristics".

127.   Ferman, Louis A. The Negro and Equal Employment Opportunities; A
Review of Management Experiences in 20 Companies. New York: Praeger,
1968.

128.   Ferman, Louis A. et al, comps. Negroes and Jobs: A Book of
Readings. Ann Arbor: University of Michigan Press, 1968.

    A collection of articles in the reformist mold discussing
    the economic status of Black Americans, causes of
    employment discrimination, the Black labor market and
    prescriptions aimed at ending employment discrimination.
    This volume contains a forward by A. Philip Randolph.

129.   Fernandez, John P. Black Managers in White Corporations. New
York: John Wiley & Son, 1975.

130.   Finney, John D. "A Study of Negro Labor During and After World
War I".   Diss. Georgetown, 1967.

    A detailed look at Afro-American industrial labor, as
    influenced by WWI.

131.   Fishback, Price. "Employment Conditions of Blacks in the Coal
Industry, 1900-1930".   Diss. University of Washington, 1983.

    Black labor is compared with native white and immigrant
    labor in the coal industry using a Schumpeterian
    competition model, in which racial discrimination is viewed
    as less important to Black labor mobility as compared to
    the acquisition of human capital.
    Specifically, wage rates in the West Virginia coal industry

were reviewed as non-discriminatory, and supports the
authors hypothesis that Blacks were not victims of
discrimination that affected their safety. A lack of
management level job opportunity for Blacks was seen as the
main form of discrimination. The study contends that
historians have overplayed the process of exploitation in
the coal industry, while overlooking the importance of the
competitive process.

132.   Fleischman, Harry and Rorty, James. We Open the Gates: Labor's
Fight for Equality. New York: National Labor Service, n.d.

An optimistic, union sponsored survey of Black labor
progress in various unions including the Steelworkers, UAW,
Textile, Railroad, Hotel and Rubber Workers Union.

133.   Fletcher, Arthur. The Silent Sell-out: Government Betrayal of
Blacks to Craft Unions. New York: Third Press, 1974.

The author presents data on the government's failure to
integrate the skilled trades.

134.   Fletcher, F. Marion. The Negro in the Drug Manufacturing
Industry. Philadelphia: Wharton School/Industrial Research Unit, 1970.
(See Northrup, Negro Employment in Basic Industry).

135.   Fletcher, F. Marion. The Negro in the Drugstore Industry.
Philadelphia: Wharton School/Industrial Research Unit, 1971. (See
Northrup, Negro Employment in Basic Industry).

136.   Fletcher, Linda P. The Negro in the Insurance Industry.   Wharton
School/Industrial Research Unit, 1970. (See Northrup, Negro Employment
in Basic Industry).

137.   Flynn, Charles L. White Land, Black Labor. Baton Rouge:
Louisiana State University Press, 1983.

Based on his dissertation, The author assumes that Southern
history is based upon the linkages and tensions between a
culturally defined caste system and an economically defined
class system. This scholarly study focuses on Georgia's
post Civil War economy and race relations and the
mechanisms which fostered Black inequality, especially in
agriculture.

138.   Flynn, Charles Lenean Jr. "White Land, Black Labor: Property,
Ideology and the Political Economy of Late Nineteenth-Century Georgia".
Diss. Duke, 1980.

Using documentary material, the author discusses racial and
land relations, caste and class values, racial
discrimination and small/middle white property owners who
intensified their reactionary and exploitative relationship
to Black agricultural laborers after the Civil War.

139.   Fogel, Walter A. The Negro in the Meat Industry. Philadelphia:
Wharton School/Industrial Research Unit, 1970. (See Northrup, Negro
Employment in Basic Industry).

140.   Foley, Eugene P.   The Achieving Ghetto.   Washington, D.C.:
National Press, 1968.

A "Hubert Humphrey Liberal" approach to economic
development in the Black ghettos of America.

141.   Foner, Philip S.   Essays in Afro-American History.   Philadelphia:
Temple University Press, n.d.

This collection of essays includes sections dealing with
the role of Blacks in the Socialist Movement, labor
movement, Black-white labor relations, skilled Black
tradesmen excluded from the labor market by immigrants, and
the IWW's struggle against racism in the labor movement.

142.   Foner, Philip S.   Organized Labor and the Black Worker, 1619-1973.
New York: Praeger, 1974.

This excellent historical overview of Black labor and trade
unionism focuses on the post Civil War period, despite its
title. The subjects include The Colored National Labor
Union, The Knights of Labor, the AFL, the IWW, the railroad
Brotherhood, the CIO, the Cold War, the Black Power
Movement in trade unions during the late 1960's and the
emergence of the Coalition of Black Trade Unionists.

143.   Foner, Philip S. and Lewis, R. L., eds . The Black Worker: A
Documentary From Colonial Times to Present. VIII Vols. Philadelphia:
Temple University Press, 1983.

The Black Worker is an eight volume series of historical
documents pertaining to the development of Black workers in
America. It is the only publication on Black workers based
upon original historical literature including newspapers,
magazines, letters, labor journals, labor achival
materials, and proceedings from various labor meetings and
events. The complex relationship of conflict and
cooperation between Black and white workers is a central
element in each volume. Each volume is indexed and
provides useful end notes. The volumes include:

Vol. I The Black Worker to 1869
Topics covered by relevant documentation include slaves as
craftsmen, industrial slaves, occupations of free Blacks in
the North and South, northern and southern industrial/race
relations, Black seamen, waiters, caulkers, the Civil War
and Reconstruction.

Vol. II The Black Worker During the Era of the National
Labor Union
This volume presents historical documents from the Colored
National Labor Union, Black and white labor relations,
Black socialism and the Greenback-labor Party, the Ku Klux
Klan and Black labor, Black migration from the south to the
north.

Vol. III The Conditions of Black Workers in the South
This volume focuses on the Knights of Labor and Black
farmer organizations. While several books and manyr3
articles have been written on the Knights, this volume
represents the only publication of historical documents
from the "Nobel Order".

Vol. IV The American Federation of Labor and the Black
Worker, 1881-1903
This volume, concerned with Black workers and the AFL,
Samuel Gompers, the machinists, bricklayers, longshoremen,
pullmans, porters, rail Brotherhood, United Mine Workers
and strikebreaking, contains unique historical
documentation.

Vol. V The Black Worker from 1900-1919
This volume concentrates on economic conditions of Black
workers, several strikes, migration and northern race
riots, and WWI in relation to Black workers.

Vol. VI The Era of Post-war Prosperity and the Great
Depression, 1920-1936
This volume contains records/letters concerning Black women
in industry, the selected correspondence between A.P.
Randolph and Milton Webster, Brotherhood of Sleeping Car
Porters, American Negro Labor Congress, The Communist
Party, and the AFL in relation to Black labor between
1920-1936.

Vol. VII The Black Worker from the Founding of the CIO to
the AFL-CIO Merger, 1936-1955
This volume covers the CIO, the Steelworkers Organizing
Committee, tobacco workers, Black seamen, The National
Negro Congress, sharecroppers, March on Washington
Movement, FEPC, the post WWII period, The National Negro
Labor Council, Paul Robeson and the AFL-CIO merger in
relation to Black workers.

Vol. VIII The Black Worker Since the AFL-CIO Merger,
1955-1980
This volume presents contemporaneous documents pertaining

to Black labor.

144.   Fonor, Eric. Nothing but Freedom: Emancipation and its Legacy.
Baton Rouge: Louisiana State University Press, 1983.

145.   Ford, David Jr. Readings in Minority Group Relations. La Jolla:
University Associates, 1976.

    A collection of scholarly articles, many dealing with the
    question of Black labor in a variety of
    organizational/industrial circumstances. Testing,
    integration, job satisfaction and prejudice are discussed
    from diverse academic orientations.

146.   Ford, James William. Economic Struggle of Negro Workers. New
York: New York Provisional International Trade Union Committee, 1930.

    The Communist Party's view, in brief, on Black labor in the
    Depression era. James Ford, a Black Communist, was also a
    party leader. The concept of Black self determination in
    the Cotton Belt is discussed.

147.   Franklin, Charles L. The Negro Labor Unionist of New York. Diss.
Columbia, 1936. Studies in History, Economics and Public Law. New York:
Columbia University Press, 1936.

    The discrimination faced by Negroes in Manhattan based
    unions is presented.

148.   Freeman, Everette J. "An Examinaton of Blacks in Union Leadership
Positions in the United States".   Diss. Rutgers, 1983.

    A unique effort to quantify the number of elected, and
    appointed Black union officials in the United States. The
    union leadership process, Black rank and file support,
    civic ties, and differences between local/national offices
    in relation to Black union officials was determined by
    utilizing a survey questionaire.

149.   Freeman, Richard B. Black Elite. New York: McGraw-Hill, 1976.

    A detailed study of the post World War II Black
    professional class (including teachers and government
    employees) in relation to employment opportunity, education
    and government intervention.
    The author optimistically assesses the market demand for
    highly trained Blacks, and argues that tremendous gains
    have been made by Blacks seeking professional employment.

150.   Friedlands, Stanley. <u>Unemployment in the Urban Core</u>. New York:
Praeger, 1972.

   An analysis of unemployment in 30 urban centers with
   orientation toward policy recommendations aimed at
   improving Black employment oppotunity, and government
   functioning.

151.   Frost, Olivia P. "A Study of the Effect of Training upon the
Level of Occupational Aspirations and upon Attitudes Toward Work for Nine
Groups of Young Negro Men from Low Income Families".   Diss. New York,
1972.

   A statistically oriented study of job attitudes of Black
   men in New York City, 1970-71. A questionaire/survey
   method was used to gather empirical evidence, creating the
   basis for the author to postulate job training and positive
   attitude reinforcement as prerequisites for upward
   mobility.

152.   Fujita, Kuniko. <u>Black Worker's Struggles in Detroit's Auto
Industry, 1935-1975</u>. Saratoga: Century Twenty One Publishers, 1980.

   A look at the status of Black workers in the auto industry,
   the UAW and the League of Black Revolutionary Workers.

153.   Fulmer, William E. <u>The Negro in the Furniture Industry</u>.
Philadelphia: Wharton School/Industrial Research Unit, 1973. (See
Northrup, <u>Negro Employment in Basic Industry</u>).

154.   Galarza, Ernesto. <u>Farm Workers and Agri-business in California,
1947-1960</u>. Notre Dame: University of Notre Dame, 1977.

   The author presents a well documented story of agricultural
   exploitation in California, with important reference to the
   status and conditions of Black and Mexican American labor.
   Contains an excellent regional bibliography.

155.   Galchus, Kenneth E. <u>The Elasticity of Substitution of White for
Non-white Labor</u>. U.S. Department of Commerce/Bureau of Standards.
Washington, D.C.: GPO, 1970.

   Multiple regression analysis is used in this economically
   oriented thesis originally written in 1970 at Washington
   University.

156.   Galloway, Lowell E. <u>Manpower Economics</u>. Homewood: Richard D.
Irwin, 1971.

   A capitalist oriented labor market analysis of various

employment factors, with some sections discussing
"non-white" and Black job discrimination.

157.   Gannett, Frank. **Minority Employment in Daily Newspapers.**
Evanston: Northwestern University, 1978.

A superficial look at daily newspapers and Black employment
and readership.

158.   Gannett, H. **Occupations of the Negro.** John F. Slater Fund
Occasional Papers, No. 6. Baltimore: John Murphy, 1895.

This work discusses the mainly agriculturally rooted labor
experiences of pre-20th century Black labor.

159.   Garfinkel, Herbert. **When Negroes March.** New York: Free Press of
Glencoe, 1959.

An examination of the planned 1941 March on Washington led
by A. P. Randolph, and a discussion of the Fair Employment
Practices Committee. The author draws linkage between
Black protest and employment policies.

160.   Gaston, John Coy. "The Denver Area Black Professional/
Businesswoman's Perception of her Communication with the Black Male".
Diss. University of Colorado at Boulder, 1979.

Fifty Black women from forty different occupations were
interviewed to determine the status of the relationship
between themselves and Black men. Their responses varied
depending upon their family and marital relations.

161.   Gatewood, Wallace Laval. "Afro-American Manpower and Affirmative
Action in High Level Occupations: 1970-80".   Diss. University of
Illinois at Urbana-Champaign, 1975.

A quantitative economic analysis of the labor supply demand
imbalance among college educated Black men in 82 high level
occupations between 1970-80. The author suggests that the
employers elimination of racial bias is necessary but not
sufficient to guarantee proportionate representation at all
occupational levels. Affirmative Action is required for
long term and fundamental institutional desegregation.

162.   Gelber, Steve. **Black Men and Businessmen.** Port Washington:
Kennikat Press, 1974.

An optimistic study of the business community's attempts to
accommodate racial integration in employment.

163.   Gershenfeld, Walter Jay. "The Negro Labor Market in Lanchester, Pennsylvania".   Diss. University of Pennsylvania, 1964.

An analysis of racial labor market participation in Lanchester, Pennsylvania, outlining barriers to equal employment.

164.   Geschwender, James. Class, Race and Worker Insurgency. Cambridge: Cambridge University Press, 1977.

The best discussion and analysis of the rise and fall of the League of Revolutionary Black Workers that first appeared in Detroit during the late 1960's. Unionism, radical politics, the Civil Rights Movement, the Dodge Revolutionary Union Movement, Black worker exploitation and militancy are presented in an historical context. Contains excellent references.

165.   Gilkes, Cheryl Louise Townsend. "Living and Working in a World of Trouble: The Emergent Career of the Black Woman Community Worker". Diss. Northeastern, 1979.

A case study and interview of 25 Black women community activists, fighting against racism and for Black economic development, detailing specific community work, conflicts, affiliations and other activities within this division of Black community labor.

166.   Gill, Gerald R. Meanness Mania. Washington, D.C.: Howard University Press, 1980.

An examination of the conservative, anti-affirmative action trend mainly in American education, with some references to employment and the well known Weber case of reverse discrimination in the steel industry.

167.   Ginzberg, Eli. Business Leadership and the Negro Crisis. New York: McGraw Hill, 1968.

Columbia University's Graduate School of Business sponsored two conferences (in 1964 and 1968) on minority economic development. The first resulted in a work entitled The Negro Challenge to the Business Community, McGraw Hill (1966) and the second resulted in the volume cited above. In the second publication, corporate oriented government officials, academicians, Blacks and business executives focused (without documentation) on Black economic development. The authors generally attempt to increase Black access to and participation in the dominant economic order.

168.   Ginzberg, Eli.   The Negro Potential.   New York: Columbia
University Press, 1956.

A survey of economic opportunity, educational preparation
and federal manpower policy as it pertains to Black labor.

169.   Glasgow, Douglas.   The Black Underclass.   San Francisco:
Jossey-Bass, 1980.

The author writing from a "Black perspective" focuses on
employment and social problems faced by 40 Black males.

170.   Glover, Dennis F.   "The Perceived Impact of Use of Legal and
Confrontation Procedures on the Continued Employment of Black Principals
in the West Central Georgia, 1968-1974".   Diss. University of Colorado,
1974.

A study of the Georgia Teachers and Education Association
attempts to prevent the elimination of Black principals in
West Georgia's desegregated schools.

171.   Goins, John B.   The American Colored Waiter.   Hotel Monthly
Handbook Series.   New York: Hotel Monthly, 1902.

At the turn of the century, a waiter's job was highly
esteemed in the Black community. This small text explores
the status of Blacks in the profession.

172.   Goldstein, Bernard.   Low Income Youth in Urban Areas.   New York:
Holt, Rinehart & Winston, 1967.

A survey of the literature and a discussion of the
conditions of youth (mainly Black) in relation to
education, employment, the government, the law, etc.

173.   Gorden, Joan L.   "Some Socio-economic Aspects of Selected Negro
Families in Savannah, Georgia: With Special References to the Effects of
Occupational Stratification on Child Rearing".   Diss. University of
Pennsylvania, 1955.

An interesting study of how occupational differences
amongst 216 Savannah families, "affects patterns of [Black]
child rearing".

174.   Gore, George W. Jr.   "Negro Public School Teachers in Tennessee".
Diss. Columbia, 1940.

A detailed look at the status of Black public school
teachers in Tennessee.

175.   Gould, William B. "Black Workers in White Unions".   Diss.
Cornell, 1977.

An outstanding legal analysis of the development of
discrimination in relation to labor-management relations
and institutional behavior. The author demonstrates the
importance of legal remedies and enforcement while
discussing specific cases and laws. Seniority, quotas,
back pay, the National Labor Relations Act, Taft-Hartley,
the construction industry and grievance arbitration
machinery in relation to Title VII of the 1964 Civil Rights
Act are among the topics covered. One of the best lists of
discrimination related legal cases in print is found at the
end of this text.

176.   Gourlay, Jack G. The Negro Salaried Worker. AMA Research Study
No. 70. New York: American Management Association, 1965.

177.   Gragnon, Carol Ann. "The Labor Movement and the Problem of
Anti-black Discrimination".   Masters thesis Florida Atlantic, 1972.

A brief look at the AFL-CIO structure and function
vis-a-vis Black workers (contains an interview with Jesse
Jackson) and discrimination.

178.   Graham, Glennon. "From Slavery to Serfdom: Rural Black
Agriculturalists in South Carolina, 1865-1900".   Diss. Northwestern,
1982.

A study of the special nature of exploitation and
oppression of South Carolina's freedman during the
Reconstruction and post Reconstruction periods. Black and
party politics are discussed in relation to white racist
suppression of the struggle for equality waged by Black
agricultural laborers who were once again reduced to
serfdom with the onset of the Black Codes in the 1880s.

179.   Grant, Robert B. The Black Man Comes to the City: A Documentary
Account from the Great Migration to the Great Depression, 1915 to 1930.
Chicago: Nelson-Hall, 1972.

A substantial portion of this study is based on the "push"
and "pull" employment factors causing Black migration from
the rural South to the urban North between 1915 and 1930.

180.   Greene, Lorenzo J. and Callis, M.C. Employment of Negroes in the
District of Columbia; Survey. Washington,D.C.: Associated Publishers,
[n.d., ca. 1933].

181.   Greene, Lorenzo J. and Woodson, Carter. <u>Negro Wage Earner.</u>
Washington, D.C.: Association for the Study of Negro Life and History,
1930.

A classic, highly detailed study of Black workers since
emancipation. The topics include agricultural labor,
domestic service, manufacturing, artisans, transportation,
apprenticeship, metal, coal and other smaller industries.
A statistical outline of the employment status during the
first third of the 20th century is presented with an
analysis of racial relations and employment discrimination
barriers. A large number of studies on Black labor cite
this work as being of fundamental significance to the
literature.

182.   Greenwald, Maurine Weiner. <u>Women, War and Work: The Impact of</u>
<u>World War I on Women Workers in the United States.</u>   Westport: Greenwood
Press, 1980.

The author looks at the impact of WWI on the nature and
structure of female (including Black employment,
government policies, labor reform, female social
contradictions vis-a-vis women and labor). Extensive
bibliography.

183.   Greer, Scott A. <u>Last Man In; Racial Access to Union Power.</u>   New
York: Free Press, 1959.

184.   Gregory, O. Grady. <u>From the Bottom of the Barrel.</u>   Chicago:
National Alliance of Postal and Federal Employees of Chicago, 1977.

A unique, brief and personal narative of the history of
Chicago's Black postal workers between 1921 and the 1960's.
Some interesting points of history, however social analysis
is absent, and often the book is over personalized.

185.   Griffin, James S. <u>Blacks in the St. Paul Police and Fire</u>
<u>Departments 1885-1976.</u>   Minneapolis: E & J, 1973.

A non-scholarly look at Black police and fire personnel in
St. Paul, Minnesota.

186.   Grimes, John J. "The Black Man in Law Enforcement: An Analysis of
the Destination of Black Men in Law Enforcement Agencies and the Related
Recruitment Problems".   Masters thesis John Jay College, 1969.

An effort to determine the factors causing
under-representation of Black law enforcement agencies.

187.   Grinnell, Gloria Claudette. "Work-related Stress Amongst Black
Female Professionals".   Diss. United States International, 1982.

The thesis focuses on the stress levels of Black women
employed as professionals in Los Angeles. Self perception,
child dependency and the race of the employer formed the
core of the 14 item questionaire survey of 120 Black women.
The author concludes that being Black, to a greater degree
than being a woman, was the most significant factor in
stress.

188.   Gross, James Augustine. "The NAACP, the AFL-CIO, and the Negro
Worker".   Diss. University of Wisconsin at Madison, 1962.

A look at the conflicts over racial policies between the
AFL and the NAACP.

189.   Haber, William. Labor in a Changing America. New York: Basic
Books, 1966.

This work contains scattered references to Black workers.
The most detailed discussion of Blacks is contained in a
chapter entitled "The Position of Minorities in the
American Labor Movement" by Ray Marshall.

190.   Haddad, William F. and Pugh, G. Douglas. Black Economic
Development. Series I. Englewood Cliffs: Prentice Hall, 1969.

A series of articles discussing different aspects of Black
economic development sponsored by the American Assembly,
Columbia University. Contributors from government,
business and academia.

191.   Hall, Charles. Negroes in the United States, 1920-1932. Bureau
of the Census. Washington, D.C.: GPO, 1935.

192.   Hall, Edgerton Elliott. "The Negro Wage Earner of New Jersey; A
Study of Occupational Trends in New Jersey, of the Effects of Unequal
Racial Distribution in the Occupations and the Implications for Education
and Guidance".   Diss. Rutgers, 1933.

The best study of early twentieth century Afro-American
occupational trends in New Jersey, with a focus on
mobility, unequal opportunity, specific occupations
including agriculture, domestic service, manufacturing and
professional services. The social implications for
housing, education, mortality, delinquency, etc., in
relation to employment discrimination are discussed.

193.   Halvorsen, Marcia. "Black-white Earning Differentials in a Rural

Southern Labor Market". Diss. Georgia State, 1978.

> The author studies wage differentials in a 1967 rural
> Georgia randon sample of 20% of the population in two
> counties. Statistics are used to explore leading
> hypotheses related to racial income differences. The
> author suggests that wage differentials are due largely to
> productivity differences between Blacks and whites. A
> useful discussion of the literature on wage differential
> precedes the case study.

194. Hamburger, Robert. A Stranger in the House. New York: Collier,
1978.

> An interview series with New York area Black maids. One of
> the few publications containing extensive biographical data
> on Black workers.

195. Hamilton, Donna Cooper. "The National Urban League During the
Depression, 1930-1939: The Quest for Jobs for Black Workers". Diss.
Columbia, 1982.

> Utilizing National Urban League records and other primary
> data, a detailed picture and analysis of the activities of
> the National Urban league during the Depression era is
> presented. Specifically, National Urban League efforts to
> gain employment for Blacks in New Deal projects, the NUL's
> relationship with organized labor, and the role of the
> NUL's decentralized structure and conservative financial
> supporters on its policies are viewed in the theoretical
> context of crisis theory and worker advocacy. The author
> suggests that the National Urban League was a pragmatic
> organization that attempted to maintain a delicate balance
> between the Black community, Black workers and
> philanthropic supporters.

196. Hampton Institute. Negro Labor Newpaper Clippings, 1900-1921.
Newpaper Clipping No. 153. VII Vols. Hampton: Peabody Collection, n.d.

197. Hampton Institute. The American Federation of Labor and the Black
Man, 1919-1920. News Clipping No. 164. Hampton: Peabody Collection,
n.d.

198. Hampton Institute. The Negro Worker in Minnesota. Pamphlet No.
997. Hampton: Peabody Collection, n.d.

199. Hancock, Allen. "The Study of Programs for Professional
Preparation of Secondary School Teachers by Negro Publicity Supported
Colleges". Diss. University of Colorado, 1951.

"A report on the professional preparation of Negro
secondary school teachers including admission to teachers
Education programs, cirriculums, etc."

200.   Hanes, Bailey C.   Bill Pickett, Bulldogger.   Norman: University of
Oklahoma Press, 1977.

Bill Pickett's biography as a relatively well known Black
cowboy in Oklahoma, is detailed, and light is shed on the
conditions of Negro people at the turn of the 19th century.

201.   Hanushek, Eric.   Sources of Black-White Earnings Differences.
Report No. 81-B7.   Stanford: Stanford University, 1981.

A brief analysis of causal factors leading to wage
discrimination.

202.   Hare, Nathaniel.   "The Changing Occupational Status of the Negro
in the United States: An Intracohort Analysis".   Diss. University of
Chicago, 1963.

203.   Harrison, Bennett.   Education, Training and the Urban Ghetto.
Baltimore: John Hopkins University Press, 1972.

The author presents a scholarly micro-analytical and
economic study of urban minority employment. Based on an
earlier dissertation, Harrison presents evidence supporting
his contention that Blacks form a secular labor market.
Theories of economic discrimination are critically
discussed including Gary Beckers' Human Capital Theory and
the dual labor market theory. Government urban employment
policy is also reviewed.

204.   Harrison, George.   Chicago Race Riots.   Chicago: Great Western,
1919.

"Dedicated to the promotion of understanding and
cooperation between the races"- written during a period of
intensive employment related strife in Chicago when white
unions were broken by Blacks who "scabbed" in order to gain
entry in urban industrialization and mass production
process.

205.   Harris, ·Abram.   The Negro Worker.   New York: National Executive
Committee/Conference for Progressive Labor Action, 1930.

A brief historical and useful document concerning Black
entree to organized labor.

206.   Harris, Abram Lincoln. <u>Abram Lincoln Harris Papers, 1914-1929.</u>
Washington, D.C.: Howard University Collection, n.d.

A prolific writer in the topic of Black labor, Harris'
papers include twenty nine items spanning the period
1914-1929 including manuscripts, pamphlets, letters,
articles, union documents, legal briefs, etc., concerning
Black labor, discrimination, socialism and the IWW.

207.   Harris, Abram Lincoln. "The Black Worker: A Study of the Negro
and the Labor Movement".   Diss. Columbia, 1931. (See Spero and Harris,
<u>The Black Worker</u>)

208.   Harris, William. <u>Keeping the Faith: A. Philip Randolph, Milton P.
Webster, and the Brotherhood of Sleeping Car Porters, 1925-1937.</u>   Urbana:
University of Illinois Press, 1977.

The best account to date of the Brotherhood and its
leadership, during the critical formation period 1925-1937.
Harris discusses the relationship between Randolph, Webster
and the NAACP, the Urban League and the Pullman Company in
connection with the Brotherhood of Sleeping Car Porters'
struggle against racial discrimination in the railroad
industry.

209.   Harris, William H. <u>The Harder We Run.</u> New York: Oxford
University Press, 1982.

A scholar's sympathetic, historic overview of the economic
and employment plight of Black workers after the Civil War.
The author outlines the historic forces and contours of
oppression faced by Black workers. Racial discrimination
based on a history of slavery, migration, unionization
(esp. the Knights of Labor, Sleeping Car Porters), the
Depression, WWII, are all discussed. Alternating periods
of Black-white unity and conflict, the Civil Rights
Movement, Negro labor radicalism, the Negro American Labor
Congress, and communism in relation to Black workers are
treated.
The author substantiates his pessimistic conclusion with an
analysis of structural unemployment due to racism, the
failure of affirmative action, and the pervasive entrenched
nature of the "color line".
The book is based on primary and secondary source material.
The footnoted sources are among the best in contemporary
Black labor literature. A useful guide to further readings
is appedexed.

210.   Hartshorn, Herbert Hadley. "Vocational Interest Patterns of Negro
Professional Men".   Diss. University of Minnesota, 1948.

A "Vocational Interest Blank" survey of 802 lawyers, 889

life insurance salesmen and 904 physicians.

211.   Hawley, Langston Thacker.   Negro Employment in Birmingham
Metropolitan Area.   Committee of the South.   Washington, D.C.: National
Planning Association, 1954.

A brief examination of Black employment in Birmingham
industry during a period of intense segregation.   Blacks
were kept out of the better jobs, but still were important
to the local economy.

212.   Hayes, Lawrence J.W.   The Negro Federal Government Worker.
Studies in the Social Sciences.   Vol. III, No. 1.   Washington, D.C.:
Howard University, 1941.

A detailed study of Black federal employees in the District
of Columbia between 1883-1938.   One of the best studies on
the subject.

213.   Haywood, Harry.   Black Bolshevic: An Autobiography of an
Afro-American Communist.   Chicago: Liberator Press, 1978.

Haywood, a Black worker, discusses developments in the
Communist Party of America from the 1920's to the 1950's.

214.   Head, Laura D.   "The Determinants of Occupational Expectations of
Urban Black High School Students".   Diss. University of Michigan, 1978.

This study is focused on low income, inner city Black
youth, and attempts to determine decisive occupational
perceptions and values leading to employment.

215.   Heaston, Patricia.   "An Analysis of Selected Role Perceptions
Among Successful Black Women in the Professions".   Diss. Northwestern,
1975.

A look at several factors (family, education, occupation,
perception, etc.) influencing attitudes among a group of
Black female professionals interviewed for this study.

216.   Helmbold, Lois R.   "Making Choices, Making Do: Black and White
Working Class Women's Lives and Work During the Great Depression".
Diss. Stanford, 1983.

Utilizing interviews conducted during the 1930's by the
Women's Bureau of the Department of Labor, New Deal era
letters from maids to Franklin D. Roosevelt, and other
data, this study discusses the increased adverse impact
that the depression had on women, especially Black women,
emotionally, physically and economically.   The day to day

lives of these women are examined as a departure from the
more quantitative assessments usually found concerning
female/Black oppression and exploitation.

217.   Hemley, David D.   "Studies in the Economics of Racial
Discrimination".   Diss. Colorado State, 1972.

Using statistical linear equations, competitive assumptions
and capital/labor models, the author explores economic
growth factors, income distribution and mobility in
relation to discrimination.

218.   Henderson, Vivian W.   The Economic Status of Negroes: in the
Nation and in the South.   Series: Towards Regional Realism No. 3.
Atlanta: Southern Regional Council, 1963.

A pessimistic assessment of Afro-American employment with a
discussion of structural reorganization in the South,
limited employment and occupational gains for Black
workers, and statistics on unequal economic/race relations
especially in the Southern United States economy.

219.   Henri, Florette.   Black Migration: Movement North 1900-1920.
Garden City: Anchor, 1975.

A detailed sympathetic look at the economic, political and
social forces underpinning Black migration from 1900 to the
end of WWI.

220.   Henry, Richard Allen.   "A Comparative Study of Intergenerational
Occupational Mobility of Negro and White Male Colege Graduates".
Diss. State University of New York, 1974.

The author focuses on factors of general occupational
mobility. This study conflicts with most other mobility
studies, as it rejects race as the major factor in
employment and barriers to Black advancement.

221.   Herbst, Alma.   The Negro in the Slaughtering and Meat Packing
Industry in Chicago.   New York: ARNO & New York Times, 1971.

A Story of Black employment in Chicago's pre-1930 meat
packing and slaughtering industry. Contains a detailed
discussion of comparative statistics, unionism, mobility,
etc., of Black workers.

222.   Herman, Melvin, comp.   Work, Youth and Unemployment.   New York:
Thomas Crowell, 1968.

The problems and solutions of youth employment, with

important sections concerning black youth, form the core of
this study.

223.   Hernden, Angelo.   Angelo Hernden Papers.   New York: Schomberg
Collection n.d.

One folder of miscellaneous papers concerning Hernden's
labor and Communist Party organizing activities, and
articles discussing his 1932 arrest in Georgia. A few
legal briefs are also included.

224.   Higgs, Robert.   Competition and Coercion.   Cambridge: Hoover
Institute/Cambridge University Press, 1977.

A survey of the economic history of Black Americans between
1865 and 1914.

225.   Hill, Herbert.   Black Labor and the American Legal System.   Bureau
of National Affairs. Washington, D.C.: GPO, 1977. Vol. I.

A scholarly, detailed study of employment discrimination
and federal anti-discriminatory policies. This two part
volume documents labor-civil rights legal cases,
legislation, legal history and the status of Black workers
in various industries. Among some of the topics in Vol. I:
The 1866 Civil Rights Acts, the New Deal and the National
Labor Relations Acts, Title VII of the 1964 Civil Rights
Act. Part II discusses the shipbuilding, national defense,
trucking and railroad industries and unions. Valuable
legal references are contained in the footnotes.

226.   Hill, Herbert.   Title VII - Equal Employment Section Civil Rights
Act of 1964.   New York: NAACP, 1965.

One of the best discussions of the historic 1964 Civil
Rights Act, which, among its principle tasks was the
establishment of the Equal Employment Opportunity
Commission (EEOC).

227.   Hill, Jean and Safford, Hanford D.   Maximizing Black Potential:
Toward the Year 2000.   Proc. of a conference on the major issues and
dilemmas of minority professional development. May 1974. Louisville:
National Consortium for Black Professional Development, 1974.

228.   Hill, T. Arnold.   The Negro and Economic Reconstruction.
Washington, D.C.: Associates in Negro Folk Education, 1937.

229.   Hogan, Lloyd.   The State of the Black Economy: Issues in Community
Revitalization.   Proceedings of the 9th Annual Symposium on the State of

the Black Economy sponsored by the National Economic Association, and the Chicago Economic Development Corporation. New Brunswick: Transaction Books, 1980.

For the most part, a Black capitalist, reformist oriented series of undeveloped policy criticisms and suggestions for Black economic development.

230. Holland, Jerome. Black Opportunity. New York: Weybright and Talley, 1969.

A non-scholarly discussion of the relationship of Blacks to the American economy. Special attention is given to the issues of Black corporate employment relations and education. Without footnotes or bibliography.

231. Hooker, Robert W. Displacement of Black Teachers in Eleven Southern States. Nashville: Race Relations Information Center, 1970.

This report discusses the negative impact of teacher desegregation upon the status of Black teachers.

232. Hoos, Ida R. Retraining the Work Force: An Analysis of Current Experience. Berkeley: University of California Press, 1967.

A survey of job retraining programs in the San Francisco Bay area. Black and minority, especially Mexican American unemployment is regarded in the context of skills deprivation as being the primary factor, rather than racial or economic factors, in the cycle of poverty.

233. Hope, John. Negro Employment in Three Southern Plants of the International Harvester Company. Washington, D.C.: National Planning Association, 1953.

234. Hope, John. The Negro in the Trenton Labor Market. Trenton: Trenton Council on Human Relations, 1954.

A survey of local Black employment trends conducted between 1953 and 1954 by the Council.

235. Houchins, Joseph R. "The Protection of Racial Minorities and Certain Excluding Practices of Organized Labor". Masters thesis Ithaca, 1934.

A look at race discrimination in trade unions and employment during the 1920's and 1930's.

236. Howard, David. "The American Negro's Dilemma: Attitudes of Negro

Professionals Toward Competition with Whites".   Diss. University of
Indiana, 1963.

An empirical look at attitudes of professional Blacks
towards competion with whites in similar professions.

237.   Howard, John C.   The Negro in the Lumber Industry.   Philadelphia:
Wharton School/Industrial Research Unit, 1970.   (See Northrup, Negro
Employment in Basic Industry).

238.   Hudson, Hosea.   Black Workers in the Deep South.   New York:
International Publishers, 1972.

An autobiographic and historical account of Hosea Hudson's
life as a southern Black worker during the 1920's, thru the
Civil Rights era. His experiences as a sharecropper,
industrial worker, steel union organizer, labor leader and
communist are conveyed in the context of pervasive racial
and political discrimination.

239.   Hughes, Jonathan Thomas.   "Jobs for Need and a Need for Jobs:
Labor Force Entry and Career Thresholds of White, Black and Hispanic
Youth Across New York State".   Diss. Columbia, 1981.

Unemployment, and labor participation of minority and white
youth in New York State, particularly in the recent period,
are delineated and statistically analyzed.

240.   Hughes, Ronald Elliott.   "Race and Social Class Consciousness
Among Black Workers: Study of Ideological Contradictions".   Diss.
University of California, 1977.

An examination of the interrelationship between race and
class consciousness of 40 Los Angeles aero-space employees,
utilizing unstructures interviews, and hypothesizing that
racial discrimination is more important than class
experiences in the formation of individual consciousness.

241.   Hunter, Gary Jerome.   "Don't Buy From Where You Can't Work: Black
Depression, 1929-1941".   Diss. University of Michigan, 1977.

One of the most detailed studies of the "Job for Negroes
Campaigns" located in major Black metropolitan areas during
the Depression. Good discussion of related literature,
useful bibliography.

242.   Hunter, Osbourne.   Labor Verses Capital, Production, Commerce and
Consumption: The North, South and the Freedman.   Hampton: Hampton
Institute/Peabody Collection, n.d.

243.   Huson, Carolyn F. and Schlitz, M.E. College, Color and
Employment: Racial Differentials in Postgraduate Employment Among 1964
Graduates of Louisiana Colleges. Chicago: National Opinion Research
Center, 1966.

An urban and educationally oriented survey of the impact of
higher education on racial employment.

244.   Jackson, Giles and Davis, D. Webster. The Industrial History of
the Negro Race of the United States. 1908; rpt. Freeport: Books for
Libraries Press, 1971.

A sympathetic treatment and survey of Afro-American history
between the Civil War and the turn of the century.
Education, employment, religion, government relations, etc.
are discussed.

245.   Jackson, Luther. Free Negro Labor and Property Holding in
Virginia, 1830-1860. New York: Russell & Russell, 1971.

A look at the economic status and social barriers of Free
Black property holders in Virginia.

246.   Jacobs, Paul. The State of the Union. New York: Antheneum, 1963.

A rank and file oriented look at the status of American
unions, especially the teamsters, and the issue of union
democracy. "The Negro Worker Asserts His Rights" most
directly discussed the Black workers, the NAACP and
employment discrimination.

247.   Jeffress, Philip W. The Negro in the Urban Transit Industry.
Philadelphia: Wharton School/Industrial Research Unit, 1970. (See
Northrup, Negro Employment in Basic Industry).

248.   Johnson, Audrey Earle. "The National Association of Black Social
Workers: Structural and Functional Assessment by Leaders and Members".
Diss. University of Denver, 1975.

An attitudinal survey of the structure and function of the
NABSW based on interviews with 210 members and leaders.

249.   Johnson, Audrey Louise. "The Perceptions and Social
Characteristics related to Occupational Mobility of Black Women and
Intraracial Assimilation of Blacks in America".   Diss. New School for
Social Research, 1977.

A demographic oriented study of the perceptions and social
characteristics of Northern born Blacks, Southern born

Blacks and West Indian Black women in New York metropolitan area. The subjects of the study see racism and sexism as enduring problems related to professional advancement.

250.   Johnson, Douglas Hershel.   "Black Employment in Black-Owned Enterprises: A Study of Internal Labor Markets".   Diss. Massachusetts Institute of Technology, 1979.

251.   Johnson, Ellsworth.   "Urban Executive Leadership Development for Black Professionals: A Research Evaluation of an Applied Behavioral Science Program".   Diss. University of California, 1970.

A theoretical and empirical study of the process of preparing Black professionals for leadership and development in Public Administration.

252.   Johnson, Keith Whitaker.   "Racial Division of Labor and the American Negro. A Statistical Study of the Occupational Distribution of the Four Major Race and Nativity Groups in the United States, With Particular Discussion of the Negro".   Diss. Duke, 1944.

"A statistical study of the occupational distribution of four major race and nationality groups in the United States..."

253.   Johnston, Randall L.   "Franklin D. Roosevelt, John F. Kennedy, Lydon B. Johnson and the Struggle for Black Equality in Employment". Hanover: Dartmouth Senior Fellowship Project, 1980.

A look at presidential policy vis-a-vis Black employment and upward mobility.

254.   Jones, Barbara.   "The Contribution of Black Women to the Income of Black Families: An Analysis of the Labor Force Participation Rates of Black Women".   Diss. Georgia State, 1973.

Family, income and employment histories of Black women are analyzed with variables to determine the participation rate of Black women as part of a family unit. An interesting survey of 945 Black wives and factors and conditions influencing their economic relationship to the family.

255.   Jones, Edward H.   Blacks in Business.   New York: Grosset & Dunlap, 1971.

256.   Jones, John Bernard.   "Role Perception, Performance and Characteristics of Selected State Associated Senior Colleges and Universities in the Commonwealth of Pennsylvania".   Diss. University of Pittsburgh, 1974.

A look at role perception, performances and other
characteristics of Black Administrators in Pennsylvania.

257.   Jones, Thomas Mac Jr.   "Some Psychological and Personal Variables
Related to the Vocational Development of Black Male Workers".   Diss.
North Carolina State, 1980.

A look at psychological and personal variables related to
the Black industrial worker including measures of employee
attitude, acculturation, job skills and aspirations.

258.   Josey, E.J.   What Black Librarians Are Saying.   Metuchen:
Scarecrow Press, 1972.

The most developed chronical of the professional opinion of
Black librarians in the U.S. ever written.   Subjects
include community relations, academic libraries, major
issues and social orientation of Black librarians.

259.   Josey, E.J. and Shockley, Ann Allen, eds.   Handbook for Black
Librarianship.   Littleton: Libraries Unlimited, 1977.

A comprehensive, scholarly overview of the state of the
library sciences in relation to Black special collections,
goals and activities of Black librarians, as perceived by a
number of professional librarians.

260.   Kasten, Richard Allen.   "Studies of Occupational Mobility for
Black and White Men".   Diss. Massachusetts Institute of Technology,
1975.

261.   Katz, William Loren.   The Black West.   Garden City: Doubleday,
1971.

An important study intended as a school text for young
people, of Black labor in the old west - including cowboys,
explorers, settlers and military men.   Outstanding
documentation, photos and graphics.

262.   Kaufman, Robert L.   "Racial Discrimination and Labor Market
Segregation".   Diss. University of Wisconsin at Madison, 1981.

An exploration of the process of differential sorting of
Black and white labor and the influences of industrial
occupational structures on sorting, utilizing 1970 public
data, samples and archival sources.
The author postulates that minimally 14% of the wage
differential between Blacks and whites is the direct result
of discrimination.   The author questions the dual economy

approach in connection with discrimination, and recommends
an increased understanding of differential sorting in
anti-discriminatory social policy.

263.   Kelsey, Carl. Evolution of Negro Labor. Publication No. 366.
Philadelphia: American Academy of Political Science, 1903.

A reactionary assessment of Black labor at the dawn of the
20th century.

264.   Kemp, Maida Springer. Maida Springer Kemp. interview.
Cambridge: Radcliffe College/Black Woman Oral History   Project, n.d.

Maida Springer Kemp of Chicago, an active trade unionist,
was a general organizer and a member of the International
Ladies Garment Workers Union and a civil rights activist.

265.   Kennedy, Louise U. The Negro Peasant Turns City Ward. New
York: Columbia University Press, 1930.

A look at early 20th century Black migration to Northern
cities with substancial sections devoted to industrial and
employment conditions.

266.   Kentucky. Commission on Human Rights. Black Restaurant Workers
are Concentrated in the Kitchens. Report No. 79. Lexington: the
Commission, 1979.

A survey report concerning specific restaurant employment
discrimination against Black workers and women in
Louisville.

267.   Kentucky. Commission on Human Rights. Kentucky's Black Teacher
Gap. Lexington: the Commission, 1974.

An analysis of teacher employment in tha state between
1954-1974.

268.   Kesselman, Louis C. The Social Politics of the FEPC. Chapel
Hill: University of North Carolina Press, 1948.

The National Council for a Permanent Fair Employment
Practice Committee's story of coalition politics and
organizational dynamics is told here. The role of Black
labor in relation to other progressive forces makes this an
important aspect in the history of the struggle to enact
federal anti-discrimination employment policy, starting in
the New Deal era of President Roosevelt.

269.   Kester, Howard. Revolt Among Sharecroppers. New York: Arno
Press, 1969.

An indepth account of the struggle of tenant farmers and
sharecroppers in the Southern Cotton Industry.

270.   Kheel, Theordore W. Guide to Fair Employment Practices.
Englewood Cliffs: Prentice-Hall, 1964.

A discussion of Federal Fair Employment laws,
discrimination against Black workers, and 11 case studies
of successful anti-discriminatory employment policy
implementation.

271.   Kidd, Foster. Profile of the Negro in American Dentistry.
Washington, D.C.: Howard, 1979.

An effort to raise the public awareness concerning the
contributions made by Blacks in the field of dentistry.
Dental schools, organizations, manufactures, suppliers,
etc., are also discussed.

272.   Kiehl, Robert Edward. Opportunities for Blacks in the Profession
of Engineering. Diss. Rutgers 1957. Newark: Foundation for the
Advancement of Graduate Study in Engineering, 1970.

A survey of post WWII employment opportunities for Black
engineers.

273.   Killingsworth, Charles Clinton. Jobs and Income for Negroes. Ann
Arbor: University of Michigan/Institute of Labor and Industrial
Relations, 1968.

A useful monograph and analysis of late 1960's Black
employment data in relation to changing labor markets,
unemployment, sources of disadvantage in the labor market
and strategies for improving the economic status of Black
workers with transfer payments, training and economic
expansion.

274.   King, Carol B. and Risher, Howard W. Jr. The Negro in the
Petroleum Industry. Philadelphia: Wharton School/Industrial Research
Unit, 1969. (See Northrup, Negro Employment in Basic Industry).

275.   King, Jonathan. Social Inequality and Labor Force Participation.
U.S. Department of Commerce. Washington, D.C.: GPO, 1973.

A statistically oriented study utilizing a linear
regression model applied to the 1970 census, comparing
Black, white, Spanish male and female labor force

partcipation, prepared under a grant from the U.S.
Department of Labor.

276.   King, William Melvin. "Ghetto Riots and the Employment of Blacks:
An Answer to the Search for Black Political Power?".   Diss. Syracuse,
1975.

This study undertakes the determination of the impact of
urban riots, especially between 1964-67, in relations to
Black employment and political power/powerlessness.

277.   Kirkpatrick, James et al. Testing and Fair Employment. New York:
New York University Press, 1968.

The authors of the monograph discuss the social, technical
and theoretical ramifications of employment testing in
relation to race and ethnicity. The literature in the
field is reviewed, five empirical studies are presented,
and limited recommendations for testing/evaluation are
made.

278.   Klotman, Phyllis R. Frame by Frame - A Black Filmography.
Bloomington: Indiana University Press, 1979.

"A compendium of titles, credits, synopsis and sources for
world-wide Black film", with annotations.

279.   Koenig, Allen E. Broadcasting and Bargaining. Madison:
University of Wisconsin Press, 1970.

This collection of articles contains employment and legal
status information relevant to Black people in the
electronic media.

280.   Kovarsky, Irving and Albrecht, William. Black Employment.
Ames: Iowa State University Press, 1970.

A monograph discussing history, law, economics and
religion, pertaining to Black employment, from an
anti-racist perspective.

281.   Koziara, Edward C. and Koziara, Karen S. The Negro in the Hotel
Industry. Philadelphia: Wharton School/Industrial Research Unit, 1969.
(See Northrup, Negro Employment in Basic Industry).

282.   Krislov, Samuel. The Negro In Federal Employment. Minneapolis:
University of Minnesota Press, 1967.

The author focuses on anti-discriminatory federal

employment programs and policies within the federal
service. Based upon interview data, the administrative
aspect of the quest for equal employment is analyzed.
Krislov suggests that equal employment in government is the
lynch pin of broader employment progress for minorities.

283.   Lacy, Dan.   The White Use of Blacks in America.   New York:
Atheneum, 1972.

A liberal non-empirical white approach to the exploitation
of Black workers. Slavery, war, the Depression, legal and
social conditions of Black people are discussed in the
context of white racism's pervasive influence. Contains a
limited bibliographic essay.

284.   Lacy, Thomas R.   "Racial Inequality in Manufacturing: Empirical
Tests of Models of Discimination".   Diss. New School for Social
Research, 1982.

A survey and empirical test of employment discrimiantion
models including neoclassical, competition, market
segmentation and radical bargaining models. Regression
analysis is used on data from 38 states to conclude that
discrimination increases profits and lowers incomes. White
workers incomes are negatively affected by discrimination
while they benefit by increased upward occupational
opportunities. Racism contributes to an anti-labor, pro
management political environment and hampers union
organizing ability, thus structurally limiting white
income. Unionism is seen as the key in determining the
influence of racism within the context of a capitalist
political economy.

285.   Landay, Eleen.   Black Film Stars.   New York: Drake Publishers,
1973.

A series of biographical sketches with photos of the major
Black American film stars from 1903 to 1972.

286.   Lane, Layle.   Layle Lane Papers, 1933-1951.   New York: Schomburg
Collection, n.d.

Layle Lane was the first Black female vice president of the
American Federation of Teachers, a principle planner of the
March on Washington, a congressional candidate for the
Socialist Party in New York. Lane also fought for the
estabishment of the Fair Employment Practices Commission.

287.   Laurentz, Robert.   "Racial/Ethnic Conflict in the New York City
Garment District".   Diss. State University of New York at Binghamton,
1980.

A detailed analysis of Black-Jewish and Puerto Rican-Jewish relations within the International Ladies Garment Workers Union. Insofar as the union's leadership has traditionally been composed of Black and Puerto Rican women, race and ethnic conflict is closely linked with gender conflict in the I.L.G.W.U.

288. Lee, Roy. "The Black Businessman: Career Patterns and Occupational Mobility". Diss. New York, 1968.

Employment trends of Black businessmen are discussed in the context of increased pressure for upward mobility.

289. Leggon, Cheryl B. "The Black Female Professional: Role Strains and Status Inconsistencies". Diss. Chicago, 1975.

The author contends in her ethnographic field study that Black women have unique problems because of the connection between race and sex discrimination. The relation between professional and female roles, women's liberation movements and perception of discrimination were determined in a survey format. Race was found to be an even greater barrier than sex in professional development.

290. Leigh, Duane E. An Analysis of the Determinants of Occupational Upgrading. Vol. I. New York: Academic Press, 1978.

An empirical study of educational, economic, social and other variables in the occupational patterns of Blacks compared to whites in America. Cencus data are utilized in testing various mobility hypotheses, especially the dual labor market and human capital theories.

291. Leone, Richard D. The Negro in the Trucking Industry. Philadelphia: Wharton School/Industrial Research Unit, 1970. (See Northrup, Negro Employment in Basic Industry).

292. Lesnett, Frederick S. "An Exploratory Review of the Effects of Various Sociological Variables and a Negative Income Tax on the Changes in Labor Supply of Urban Black Males". Diss. Perdue, 1975.

A study of 437 Black male family heads in the Gary (Indiana) income maintenance program, and the labor supply of lower class Black men.

293. Leventhal, Sharon. Job Discrimination is Illegal: A Guide to Legal Action. No. 400. New York: Twentieth Century Fund, n.d.

A short hand guide to antidiscriminatory and pro civil

rights legal redress.

294.   Levison, Andrew.   The Working Class Majority.   New York: Penguin,
1974.

An explanation of working class political attitudes in the
post-Watergate era of the 1970's.   Some good discussion of
Black-white labor relations and the status of Black workers
in the union.

295.   Levithan, Sar et al.   Still a Dream.   Cambridge: Harvard Press,
1975.

Significant portions of this book are devoted to reviewing
and synthesizing 1970 census data, and more specialized
studies relating to Black economic development in the
context of income, employment and education.   More general
discussion of economic development in relation to health,
family, housing and institutional power/control are
presented and are often linked directly and indirectly to
employment.   Policy analysis and recommendations are
presented in the hope of overcoming barriers to equality.

296.   Levy, Frank.   Have Black Men Gained Employment?.   New York: Ford
Foundation Urban Institute, 1980.

A statistical assessment of Black employment based upon
census data that suggests a small percentage of Black
workers are making 'significant gains' while most are
regressing.

297.   Lewis, Edward.   The Mobility of the Negro.   New York: Columbia
University Press, 1931.

A useful economic and labor supply oriented analysis of
Black migration during the first quarter of the 20th
century.   The geographic distribution of Black farmers,
comparisons between white and Black farmers, the importance
of cotton and related economic factors, (prices, yield,
Boll Weevil damage, etc.), are outlined as are agricultural
and industrial trends.

298.   Library of Congress.   Brotherhood of Sleeping Car Porters Records.
Washington, D.C.: Manuscript Division, n.d.

One of the most extensive collections of Brotherhood
records is held at the Library of Congress.

299.   Library of Congress.   Carter Godwin Woodson Collection, 1875-1950.
Washington, D.C.: Manuscript Division, n.d.

Woodson, founder of Negro History Week in 1926, wrote
extensively on the topic of labor. During the early 20th
century, he was the lone voice of
consequence in Afro-American historography.

300.   Library of Congress. NAACP Legal Defense and Educational Fund
Records. Washington, D.C.: Manuscript Division, n.d.

The Defense Fund's Records contain numerous legal cases
challenging employment discrimination.

301.   Library of Congress. NAACP Records. Washington, D.C.: Manuscript
Division, n.d.

The NAACP records contain numerous references to Black
labor.

302.   Library of Congress. National Urban League: Southern Regional
Office Records. Washington, D.C.: Manuscript Division, n.d.

The Urban League Southern Regional Record, contains
numerous references to Black employment in the South, and
efforts to combat discrimination.

303.   Library of Congress. National Urban League Washington Bureau
Records. Washington, D.C.: Manuscript Division, n.d.

The Urban League Washington Bureau Records contain numerous
references to working and employment conditions of Blacks
in the United States, and various programs to overcome
employment discrimination.

304.   Library of Congress. Samuel H. Clark Papers. Washington, D.C.:
Manuscript Division, n.d.

Samuel H. Clark was a railroadman and labor leader.

305.   Library of Congress. The Division of Negro Economics, 1918-21.
Washington, D.C.: GPO., n.d.

Institutional records of the defunct Division of Negro
Economics with agricultural and industrial data.

306.   Library of Congress. The Division of Negro Labor, 1934-37.
Washington, D.C.: GPO., n.d.

Important records, statistical surveys and industrial
records pertaining to Black employment are maintained at

the Library of Congress.

307.   Library of Congress. The "Negro" Division of the United States
Employment Services. USES 1918. Washington, D.C.: GPO, n.d.

   Early 20th century governmental agency records relating
   mainly to Black agricultural employment.

308.   Lichtenstein, Jules. "White Ethnic and Black Economic
Assimilation and Mobility: A Study of Employment Patterns and
Determinants in Selected SMSA's".   Diss. Cornell, 1975.

   A discussion of ethnic and racial economic integration in
   American labor markets. Historical and quantitative
   analysis are used with regression anaylsis. Policy
   implications are discussed. The author considers the
   public sector as holding the greatest opportunity for Black
   economic advancement.

309.   London, Arcenia P. "Determinants of Self-acceptance of Black
Female School Teachers Selected From the Syracuse Public School System".
Masters thesis Syracuse, 1979.

310.   Longsworth, Polly. I, Charlotte Forten, Black and Free. New
York: Cromwell, 1970.

   A re-creation of Miss Forten's experience in the
   post-slavery era.

311.   Lutterbie, Patricia Hasen. "Occupational Patterns of Educators
Who Were Principals of Negro Schools in Florida in 1960".   Diss.
University of Miami, 1973.

   A collection of interview and statistical data presented to
   give a picture of the year to year status and conditions of
   Black Florida educators, paticularly as related to school
   desegregation.

312.   Lyle, Jerolyn R. Differences in the Occupational Standing of
Black Workers Among Industries and Cities. U.S. Equal Employment
Opportunity Commission. Washington, D.C.: GPO, 1970.

   An examination of occupational parity of Black men and
   women in 46 private sector labor markets (cities). A
   useful bibliography is included.

313.   MacDonald, Stephen, ed. Business and Blacks. Princeton: Dow
Jones, 1968.

A pro big business look at corporate efforts to promote
racial equality in employment and investment. Editors from
the Wall Street Journal have assembled a collection of
unscholarly, unsubstantiated articles on Blacks and the
American economy.

314.   Madison, Alfred Morgan. "On Being the First Black Administrator
in an Elementary School District".   Diss. United States International,
1970.

An indepth study of a Black male administrator in Chula
Vista, California.

315.   Mapp, Edward. Directory of Blacks in the Performing Arts.
Metuchen: Scarecrow Press, 1978.

A listing of Black American cultural workers in the
performing arts which details career data, family
information, professional associations, etc.

316.   Marable, June Morehead. "The Role of Women in Public School
Administration as Perceived by Black Women Administrators in the Field".
Diss. Miami, 1974.

The objective of this study was to determine the status of
female administrators, as perceived by 127 Black woman who
are field administrators.

317.   Marshall, F. Ray and Briggs, Vernon M. Jr. The Negro and
Apprenticeship. Baltimore: John Hopkins Press, 1967.

The authors' intent was to evaluate post-1960 American
apprenticeship programs with regard to the position of
Black labor within the apprenticeship process. Historical,
regional, demographic, legal and political considerations
are made along with suggestioned improvements of the
apprenticeship system. Ten major cities were special
targets in which over 100 interviews on the issue of
apprenticeship were conducted.

318.   Marshall, Ray. Labor in The South. Cambridge: Harvard University
Press, 1967.

A detailed description of the development of the trade
union movement in the South, with major references and
sections devoted to Black labor. This study is important
insofar as it is one of a very few that analyzes Black
labor in relation to union and political factors in the
South.

319.   Marshall, Ray. The Negro and Organized Labor. New York: John
Wiley & Sons, 1965.

    The author attempts to outline the development of Black and
labor movement relations in America, especially relations
between Blacks and the AFL-CIO. Race prejudice in unions,
and public policy influences (including the Fair Employment
Practice Committee and the National Labor Relations Board)
on union racial practices are examined. Confidential
interviews as well as public records comprise the bulk of
the research data base. Analysis is limited to a
systematicly oriented micro-social critique. Useful
footnotes with primary and secoundary research sources at
the end of each chapter are contained herein.

320.   Marshall, Ray. The Negro Worker. New York: Random House, 1967.

    The Negro Worker sets out to understand "the underlying
factors influencing Negro employment". Slavery, the Civil
War and Reconstruction's influences on Negro occupational
patterns are introduced to understand contemporary labor
relations in a historical context. Racial policies of the
National Labor Union, The American Federation of Labor, and
the CIO are explored. Southern racial attitudes are
discussed in connection with employment discrimination, and
the Civil Rights upsurge of the 1950's and 60's. In
analyzing Black income, education, employment and labor
force participation, the author "attempts to show that the
Negro employment problems are caused by a complex
constellation of problems and not simply by
discrimination".

321.   Marshall, Ray and Briggs, Vernon Jr. Equal Apprenticeship
Opportunities.   University of Michigan/Institute of Labor and Industrial
Relations n.d.

    A brief look at Black apprenticeship in the United States,
especially in New York city.

322.   Marshall, Ray and Christino, Virgil Jr. Employment of Blacks in
the South. Austin: University of Texas Press, 1978.

    In a collection of essays, the authors attempt to outline
the status of Black employment in the South, explore
employment factors, and prescribe policies intended to
ameliorate the pattern of Black employment in that region.
Extensive use of Equal Employment Opportunity Commission
data was made. The authors give an historical account of
Black labor in relation to agriculture, while discussing
broader social and theoretical considerations.

323.   Marshall, Ray and Godwin, Lamond. Cooperatives and Rural Poverty

in the South. Baltimore: John Hopkins Press, 1971.

This monograph analyzes southern Negro rural agricultural
employment, farm cooperatives, rural development and
government policy.

324.   Martin, Oscar Baker. A Decade of Negro Extension Work, 1914-1924.
(U.S. Department of Agriculture, Miscellaneous Circular, No. 72)
Washington, D.C.: GPO, 1926.

325.   Martin, William H. "The Development and Appraisal of a Proprietor
for Promoting The In-service Professional Improvement of Negro Teachers".
Masters thesis Ohio State, 1944.

A review of the in-service professional improvement efforts
in Dunbar High, Little Rock, Arkansas between 1943-44.

326.   Maryland. Commission on Human Relations. Racial Discrimination
in Maryland's Employment Agency. Baltimore: the Commission, 1969.

A review of discrimination faced by Blacks in the Maryland
Department of Employment Security.

327.   Masters, Stanley H. Black-white Income Differentials. Institute
for Research on Poverty Monograph Services. New York: Academic Press,
1975.

A scholarly economic study of Black-white income
differentials utilizing regression analysis, which
reinforces the theoretical supposition of multiple factors
are central to the phenomema of underpaid Black labor. The
author discusses recent theories of racial wage
differentials, while making policy recommendations for
Affirmative Action.

328. Master in Business Administration. Blacks in Business. Vol. 5, No.
5. New York: MBA Enterprises, 1971.

329.   Mayhew, Leon H. Law and Equal Opportunity. Cambridge: Harvard
University Press, 1968.

A sociological descriptive analysis of the Massachusetts
Commission Against Discrimination between 1959 and 1963.
The problems of Civil Rights and state regulations are
woven with sociological theory and history. Useful data is
presented on employment, housing and institutional
discrimination in Massachusetts, especially the
metropolitan Boston area.

330.   Mays, Benjamine E.   <u>Born to Rebel</u>.   New York: Schribners, 1971.

Mays discusses his life and times, and sheds light on the
condition of Black labor in the South, and the oppressive
status of pullman porters.

331.   McCall, John.   <u>Income Mobility, Racial Discrimination and Economic
Growth</u>.   Lexington: Lexington Books, 1973.

An economic, statistical and mathematical model oriented
study of the interrelationship between poverty and racial
discrimination - longitudinal income mobility analysis
forms the basis of the authors unique approach and theories
of employment discrimination are detailed. Economic policy
is discussed in relation to growth and upward mobility of
the impoverished strata.

332.   McClain, Freddie.   "Correlates of Job Satisfaction of Black
Superintendents".   Diss. University of Michigan, 1974.

A look at 4 major variables relating to job satisfaction.

333.   McDonald, Jessyna La'Telthia McCree.   "An Analysis of The
Relationship Among Factors Which May Influence The Occupational Mobility
of Black Personnel Within Recreation, Parks and Leisure Services".
Diss. University of Maryland, 1981.

334.   McLaurin, Benjamin.   <u>Benjamine McLaurin Papers</u>.   New York:
Schomburg Collection, n.d.

One of the most extensive documentary collections on Black
labor in America reflecting the activities of the
Brotherhood of Sleeping Car Porters, the FEPC and the Negro
American Labor Council. McLaurin was the eastern zone
supervisor of the BSCP, a Civil Rights activist, a leader
in the New York State Liberal Party and National Secretary
of the 1942 March on Washington movement leading to the
formation of the FEPC.

335.   McLaurin, Benjamin.   <u>Oral History Transcript</u>.   New York: Columbia
University/Oral History Collection, n.d.

This detailed oral history covers McLaurin's activities as
a leader in the Brotherhood of Sleeping Car Porters. In
addition, his family history is detailed as are his other
organizational activities.

336.   McLaurin, Melton.   <u>Paternalism and Protest</u>.   Westport: Greenwood,
1971.

A detailed, scholarly discussion of Southern cotton mill
workers and their efforts to organize between 1875 and
1905.

337.   McMillan, Robert Allan.   "Dual Labor Market: The Case of the Urban
Ghetto Negro Male".   Diss. University of California at Berkeley, 1972.

338.   Meier, August and Rudwick, Elliott.   Black Detroit And The Rise of
The UAW. New York: Oxford University Press, 1979.

   The author seeks to document the relationship between the
   Black community, the auto industry and the United
   Automobile Workers (UAW). The introduction of Blacks into
   the auto industry between 1917-1937, the transformation of
   Black opinion from anti-to-pro unionism, the rise of the
   CIO with the help of Black workers, Black strike breaking,
   the 1941 Ford strike, the NAACP's relationship with
   organized labor, and Black-white union relations are
   examined in detail.
   Useful bibliography in essay and footnote form, with
   primary and secondary sources of information regarding
   Black auto workers are contained herein.

339.   Michalak, Thomas J.   Economic Status and Conditions of the Negro.
Bloomington: Indiana University Focus/Black America, 1969.

   A limited, unannotated bibliographical listing of titles
   relating to the economic status of Black Americans.

340.   Microfilm Corporation of America.   Southern Tenant Farmers Union
Papers 1934-1970 and Green Rising, 1910-1977: A Supplement.   Sanford: the
Corporation, n.d.

   "STFU Papers, 1934-1970"

   "The Southern Tenant farmers Union (STFU) was formed in
   1934 under the auspices of the Socialist Party of America.
   The STFU was a response to unanticipated consequences of
   the New Deal's farm subsidy program."
   "From the outset, the STFU's membership consisted of black
   and white sharecroppers from the cotton plantations of
   eastern Arkansas. Under the leadership of H.L. Mitchell,
   Howard Kester and others, the STFU broadened its scope to
   include the Cotton Belt and the Southwest. Eventually it
   became involved in the plight of migrant sugar plantation
   and dairy workers as well as fishermen in Louisiana."

   "Clyde Johnson Papers"

   "Documented is the life of Clyde Johnson - dedicated trade
   unionist who was the last secretary of the Alabama
   Sharecroppers Union. Featured is an unpublished thesis by

Dale Rosen which documents the facts surrounding the
Reeltown Massacre, as well as Johnson's oral history."

"David S. Burgess Papers"

"Insight into the lives of migrant workers during the
1940's can be gathered through the papers of David Burgess
- a minister who saved the homes of 600 families in the
Delmo Labor Homes Project of Southeast Missouri. In later
years, Burgess was a CIO organizer and head of the Georgia
CIO."

341.   Miller, Herman P. Progress and Prospects for the Negro Worker.
Los Angeles: UCLA/Institute of Government and Public Affairs, 1964.

A brief generalized discussion of the relative and absolute
status of Black workers.

342.   Mindiola, Tatcho Jr. "The Cost of Being Mexican-American and
Black in Texas, 1960-1970".   Diss. Brown, 1978.

A unique comparative analysis of the discrimination faced
by Black and Mexican Americans with special emphasis on
labor.

343.   Mississippi. Employment Security Commission. Labor Market
Information for Affirmative Action Programs. Jackson: the Commission,
1978.

A numerical and statistical tabulation concerning
employment patterns in Mississippi.

344.   Mitchell, H.L. Mean Things Happening in this Land: The Life and
Times of H.L. Mitchell, Cofounder of the Southern Tenant Farmers Union.
Montclair: Allenheld, 1979.

A personalized account of the organizational dynamics of
the STFU. Considered to be the best book on the subject of
the agrarian rebellion which brought poor Black and white
tenant farmers together in a mass movement for economic and
political reform in the South. Contains a forward by
Michael Harrington.

345.   Mitchell, Roxanne and Weiss, Frank. A House Divided: Labor and
White Supremacy. New York: United Labor Press, 1981.

A broad discussion of racism in the ranks of organized
labor.

346.   Moore, Archie B. "A Description of the Effects of School

Desegregation on Black Secondary Principals in Alabama".   Diss. Kansas
State, 1974.

   A description of 173 Black secondary school principals
   pertaining to employment status and conditions of labor in
   a period of desegregation.

347.   Morgan State University. The Emmett J. Scott Collection.
Baltimore: Morris A. Soper Library, n.d.

   This collection contains information on Black employment
   during WWI.

348.   Morgan, John and Van Dyke, Richard. White Collar Blacks.   New
York: American Management Association, 1970.

   Management's view of recruitment, training and promotion
   for Black salaried workers thru the eyes of successful
   corporate Blacks. Unscholarly and simplistic.

349.   Morrison, Allan. Allan Morrison Papers. New York: Shomburg
Collection, n.d.

   The life of a Black journalist in 20th century urban
   America.

350.   Morrison, Nathan. Profile of the Black Physician. Englewood
Cliffs: Prentice-Hall, 1977.

   A pamphlet that statistically summarizes the employment of
   Blacks in health occupations, medical schools and the
   health care experience of Black Americans (mortality,
   insurance, hospital stays, etc.).

351.   Morrison, Richard. "Occupational Opportunities in Agricultural
and Related Fields and Their Implications for Agricultural Education of
Negro Students".   Diss. University of Michigan, 1954.

   A survey of 299 Black agricultural-vocational teachers
   concerning job opportunities and regional variations in
   agriculture, and necessary levels of training for
   employment success.

352.   Morse, Dean W. Pride and Prejudice. Montclair: Osmun Allanheld,
1980.

   By utilizing the interview method, the author focuses on
   the labor experiences of several older Black men and women,
   and contrasts their experiences with several young Puerto
   Rican men and women. While this study is non-theoretical

and involves little discussion of relevant literature,
nevertheless, it is useful in conveying a personal sense of
minority labor oppression in 20th century America.

353. Mulzac, Hugh. A Star to Steer By. New York: International
Publishers, 1963.

An autobiographical account of a Black Seamen - Captain
Hugh Mulzac - who was the first Black man to become a
ship's captain in U.S. history.

354. Mundy, Paul. "The Negro Boy Worker in Washington, D.C.".   Diss.
Catholic University of America, 1951.

A superficial study of the "boy" worker's conditions, role,
status and discriminatory position in the District of
Columbia.

355. Myers, John. "Black Human Capital: The Freedmen and the
Recontruction of Labor in Alabama 1860-1880".   Diss. Florida State,
1974.

This thesis looks at the relationship between Black workers
and the State of Alabama between 1860 and 1880. The
reorganization of post-Civil War Black labor and its impact
on free Blacks is explored in detail, as are federal
agencies, laws, positions, etc. pertaining to Black
workers.

356. Myers, Robin and Brooks, Thomas. Black Builders. New York:
League for Industrial Democracy, n.d.

A description of the Joint Apprenticeship Program of the
Workers Defense League connected with the A. Philip
Randolph Educational Foundation Fund.

357. NAACP Labor Department. Racism within Organized Labor: A Report
of Five Years of the AFL-CIO, 1965-1960. This is a staff report
reviewing conditions previously cited by the NAACP, but summarized here
at the end of five years of the merged AFL-CIO. Delivered by Herbert
Hill, NAACP Labor Secretary, at the Association"s annual meeting, January
3, 1961, New York City, New York. New York: the Association, 1961.

358. NAACP Labor Department. The Negro Wage-earner and Apprenticeship
Training Programs. New York: the Association, 1961.

A critical analysis of apprenticeship programs, social
barriers to equal opportunity and recommendations for
programmatic and policy improvement.

359.   National Committee Against Discrimination in Housing. The Impact of Housing Patterns on Job Opportunities. Washington, D.C.: GPO, 1968.

A look at the relationship between housing and employment among Blacks and other minorities.

360.   National Industrial Conference Board. Company Experience with Negro Employment. 2 Vols. New York: the Board, 1966.

Twelve case studies examining Black employment problems and practices as viewed by corporate executives.

361.   National Negro Congress. National Negro Congress Records. New York: Schomburg Collection, n.d.

362.   National Negro Congress. Negro Workers After the War. New York: the Congress, 1945.

A report about the status and efforts to improve the conditions of Black workers at Sperry Gyroscope Company in Brooklyn during the post-WWII period. A coalition composed of the National Negro Congress, the NAACP, and the United Electrical, Radio and Machine Workers Local 1224, led the struggle to integrate the plant, and reflected similar industrial/racial conflicts.

363.   National Planning Association. Committee of the South. Selected Studies of Negro Employment in the South. Case Study No. 4. Washington, D.C.: the Association, 1955.

A collection of 6- studies on Black employment in the South including Birmingham, Little Rock, New Orleans and Chattanooga.

364.   National Urban League. Ever Widening Horizons. New York: the League, 1951.

A discussion of the Urban League's vocational opportunity campaigns in the post WWII period.

365.   National Urban League. Special Policy Report on the Socio-economic Status of Blacks. New York: the League, 1976.

A very brief summary and discussion of Black unemployment.

366.   National Urban League. Department of Research and Community Projects. Negro Membership in American Labor Unions. 1930; rpt. New York: Negro Universities Press, 1969.

A qualitative and quanitative assessment of Black union
membership in national, federal, trade and independent
"Negro Unions", etc., before 1930. This text is one of the
best of its kind.

367.   Negro Labor Committee. Negro Labor Committee, 1925-1964. New
York: Schomburg Collection, 1971.

The NLC was preceded by the Trade Union Committee
for Organizing Negro Workers - 1925, and the Harlem Labor
Committee 1934.
The NLC leaders were trying to organize the most exploited
sector of labor: a) to improve the conditions of Black
workers, b) to prevent Black workers from being used as
strike breakers (which is one of the reasons established
trade unions supported them) and c) to prevent the
Communist Party and Communist ideology from gaining
organizational and ideological influence among Black
workers. At its height it represented 1/4 million Black
and white workers. The NLC received active support from
the Socialist Party.
Among the 18,500 items are:
        a.   the personal papers of Frank R. Crosswaith,
founder and long-time chairman, socialist and organizer for
the I.L.G.W.U. and who helped organize mechanics, sleeping
car porters, grocery clerks, etc. He wrote a regular
column, "Looking Around and Beyond", for Black newspapers.
        b.   office files - historical and administrative
        c.   press releases from the Negro Labor News Service
1935-1951
        d.   lists of over 150 individual unions affiliated
with the NLC in the 1930's
and 1940's.

368.   Newell, Barbara. Chicago and the Labor Movement.
Urbana-Champaign: University of Illinois Press, 1961.

A detailed history, focused on the 1930's, of trade
unionism in Chicago. A few important references to Blacks,
especially in clothing, meat packing, and steel industries.
Excellent, specialized bibliographic references.

369.   Newman, Debra, comp. Selected Documents Pertaining to Black
Workers Among the Records of the Department of Labor and Its Component
Bureaus, 1902-1964. National Archives and Record Service. Washington,
D.C.: GPO, 1977.

This volume is one of the best documents on governmental
records, New Deal agencies, industries, race relations,
legislation, Black women and other archival material
relating to Black workers. Most of the documents cited
were produced between 1918 and 1940 and include a wide

range of materials (letters, press clippings, photographs,
tape recodings, etc.)

370.   Newman, Dorothy and Steffers, Robert.   "Occupational Attainment of
Ethnic Groups and Women in 15 Industries".   Washington, D.C.: National
Urban League, 1971.

An EEOC sponsored research project, carried out
in cooperation with the Urban League, surveying particular
basic industries with regard to racial and gender
employment patterns, with a special focus on the year 1969.

371.   Newman, Dorothy K. et al.   Protest, Politics and Prosperity.   New
York: Pantheon, 1978.

A multi-disciplinary approach, and critical analysis of
Black progress in America's social and economic
institutions.   Political power, prejudice, education and
trade unionism are discussed as factors influencing
economic and social participation.

372.   Newton, James E. and Lewis, Ronald L.   The Other Slaves.   Boston:
G.K. Hall, 1978.

A scholarly collection of articles concerning
non-agricultural anti-bellum Black labor including
artisans, craftsmen, miners, mechanics, ironworkers, etc.,
with contributions from DuBois, Locke, Wesley and others.

373.   New York State.   Chamber of Commerce.   New Careers in Private
Industry.   Proc. of a joint conference of the New York Urban League and
the New York Chamber of Commerce 1968.   Albany: the Chamber, 1968.

A brief look at new job opportunities in the private sector
during the late 1960's.

374.   New York State.   Commission Against Discrimination.   Apprentices,
Skilled Craftsmen and the Negro.   Albany: the Commission, 1960.

A look at the status of non-whites in the skilled trades
especially as related to discriminatory factors in
apprenticeship, and policy consideration.

375.   New York State.   Commission for Human Rights.   Investigation of
Charges of Discriminating Practices in the New York State Employment
Services.   New York: the Commission, 1960.

A highly focused study of New York State government
employment agencies and equal employment within these
services.

376. New York State. Committee on Discrimination and Employment. The Negro Integrated. New York: New York State War Council, 1945.

A look at New York State's war industries and the issue of employment discrimination.

377. New York University. Robert F. Wagner Labor Archives. New York: the University, n.d.

Among the collections in this major labor achive pertaining to Black workers are included the papers of: Social Service Employee Union Local 371, AFSCME; District 65, UAW; New York Metro Area Postal Union, APWU; Philip Weightmen (civil rights and labor activist); Local 1-5 Department Store Workers Union, RWDSU; Ed Welsh papers (leader in the AFL-CIO); oral histories of some Black labor leaders and workers. The Tamiment Library (connected to the Archives) has material including many pamphlets concerning Blacks and the socialist left interspersed with other collections.

378. Nipson, Annie. Annie Nipson. Interview. Cambridge: Radcliffe College/Black Woman Oral History Project, n.d.

Annie Nipson of Clearfield, Pennsylvania, is a housewife and domestic worker from North carolina who was a migrant to the North.

379. Noble, Gil. Black is the Color of my Tube. Seacacus: Lyle Stuart, 1981.

An interesting insider's view of the television industry in relation to Black subject matter and employment as recanted by New York's well known Black commentator, Gil Noble.

380. Noble, Peter. The Negro in Films. Port Washington: Kennikat Press, 1969.

A review of Black film artists, the film industry, racial barriers and stereotypes therein.

381. Norgren, Paul and Hill, Samuel. Toward Fair Employment. New York: Columbia University Press, 1964.

A policy and administrative approach to the problem of fair employment with emphasis on economic trends, and analysis of federal, state and local government employment practices. Unions, the armed forces, and Fair Employment Commissions are also discussed with regard to Black participation.

382.   Norgren, Paul et al. Employing the Negro in American Industry: A
Study of Management Practices. New York: Industrial Relations
Counselors, 1959.

> A discussion of management policy and practice in employing
> Black labor, written from the corporate point of view.
> Contains a preface from Vice President Richard M. Nixon.

383.   Northrup, Herbert. Negro Employment in Basic Industry.
Philadelphia: Wharton School/Industrial Research Unit, 1970.

> The most comprehensive statistical and historical analysis
> of industrial structure, occupational distribution, wages,
> unionization of Black workers in the auto, steel, rubber,
> chemical and aerospace industries in America. Union,
> management and government policies are discussed in
> relation to larger questions of employment mobility,
> Affirmative Action, economic trends, World War II, regional
> peculiarities and civil/labor rights. Negro Employment in
> Basic Industry is the first and best known work in a series
> on Black labor.
> Limited footnotes, with special industrial focus for each
> section.
>
> Between 1970 and 1974 the research unit of the University
> of Pennsylvania's Wharton School of Finance published 31
> studies on Black workers in diverse sectors of American
> industry. This series of studies is the most extensive
> undertaking in the literature on Black labor in America.
> The 31 studies were published separately, and most are also
> grouped in several major volumes. The volumes include:
>
> Vol. I Negro Employment in Basic Industry (auto,
> aerospace, steel, rubber, petroleum and chemical
> industries)
>
> Vol. II Negro Employment in Finance (banking, insurance)
>
> Vol. III Negro Employment in Public Utilities
>
> Vol. IV Negro Employment in Southern Industry (paper,
> lumber, tobacco, coal, textile)
>
> Vol. V Negro Employment in Land and Air Transport (rail,
> air transport, trucking, urban transport)
>
> Vol. VI Negro Employment in Retail Trade (department
> store, drugstore, supermarket)
>
> Vol. VII Negro Employment in Maritime (shipbuilding,
> longshore, offshore)
>
> Vol. VIII Negro Employment in Construction

These studies written by more than 20 authors, are
essentially economic in character. Sociological references
are grounded with an economic orientation. Most of the
related studies were combined into single volumes for the
purpose of comparison. Some of the original studies have
been updated since they first appeared. Dramatic shifts in
investment, technology and industrial structure have
transformed many of the industries studied, and
consequently the position of Black workers has changed,
often significantly, in these transformed industries.
However, current research, in any comparable scope, has yet
to be done. This essential, encyclopedic series
constitutes the core of the traditional literature on Black
workers. This Ford Foundation funded research represents
the establishment's most serious, extensive effort to
understand Black labor's role in key segments of the United
States' economy.
While some of the studies of Black workers in various
industries are less detailed and developed than others, all
have a similarity of structure, quality and content.
Quanitative statistical data, used to delineate the
position of Black workers in particular sectors, and tends
to be a composite (ie. historic cummulative) descriptive
snap shot of particular branches of industry. Public
policy is given an important position in these studies
insofar as legislation, executive or judicial policy
impacts upon a given industry.
While critical of overt manifestations of discrimination,
and supportive of Affirmative Action and labor/civil
rights, systemic analysis is largely avoided. Criticism of
unions, government policy and industry is based almost
exclusively on reformist economic assumptions.
The conclusion of these studies generally denote limited
but real progress of blacks in most, but not all
industries. The general decline in the maritime industry
during the period Volume VII was published, is one of the
most notable exception to the general progress of Black
workers. Based upon the weight of statistical data
projected over time, the studies conclude that significant
discriminatory barriers and wage differentials exist at
most levels of specific industrial structures.
One can holistically and theoretically consider that if
each part of an economic system is flawed, it is safe to
conclude that the system itself is the source of the
various related flaws in smaller economic sectors.
Something inherent in the economic organization of society
and industry, is the causal factor perpetuating racial
discrimination. One may then conclude, based on the data
in these studies, that private ownership of manufacturing,
transportation, finance, etc. is the root cause of both
class and race inequity. The tendency of discrimination to
dominate every individual branch of industry, and
collectively to become the dominant discriminatory social
tendency, is rooted in economic organization and behavior.

Thus, economic discrimination has been elevated to a "law"
of socio-historic development, as demonstrated by the
Wharton School of Finance's Negro Employment Series.
All of the studies are indexed and oriented from the
approach taken by Northrup in the first volume. The first
volume contains a number of hypothesis and methodological
approaches that enable the authors to evaluate the
employment of Black labor.
In its totality of analysis of regional and institutional
race and sex bias in employment, seniority, EEOC data,
etc., a complex pattern of economic struggle is depicted.
major differences in racial/employment patterns within and
between industrial sectors are outlined.

384.   Northrup, Herbert.   "Negro Labor and Union Policies in the South".
Diss. Harvard, 1943.

385.   Northrup, Herbert.   The Negro and Employment Opportunity: Problems
and Practices.   Proc. of a conference sponsored by the Labor Relations
Council of the Wharton School of Finance and Commerce, University of
Pennsylvania.   November 13, 1964.   Ann Arbor: University of
Michigan/Bureau of Industrial Relations, 1965.

A collection of scholarly articles exploring income
differentials, equal employment opportunity legislation,
union racial practices, training, and racial conditions in
a number of specific locations and industries.

386.   Northrup, Herbert R.   The Negro in the Aerospace Industry.
Philadelphia: Wharton School/Industrial Research Unit, 1968.   (See
Northrup, Negro Employment in Basic Industry).

387.   Northrup, Herbert R.   The Negro in the Automobile Industry.
Philadelphia: Wharton School/Industrial Research Unit, 1986.   (See
Northrup, Negro Employment in Basic Industry).

388.   Northrup, Herbert R.   The Negro in the Paper Industry.
Philadelphia: Wharton School/Industrial Research Unit, 1969.   (See
Northrup, Negro Employment in Basic Industry).

389.   Northrup, Herbert R.   The Negro in the Tobacco Industry.
Philadelphia: Wharton School/Industrial Research Unit, 1970.   (See
Northrup, Negro Employment in Basic Industry).

390.   Northrup, Herbert Roof.   Organized Labor and the Negro.   New York:
Mamaroneck, 1971.

391.   Northrup, Herbert R. and Batchelder B.   The Negro in the Rubber

Tire Industry. Philadelphia: Wharton School/Industrial Research Unit, 1969. (See Northrup, Negro Employment in Basic Industry).

392.   Northrup, Herbert R., et. al. The Negro in the Air Transport Industry. Philadelphia: Wharton School/Industrial Research Unit, 1971. (See Northrup, Negro Employment in Basic Industry).

393.   North Carolina. Good Neighbor Council. Employment in State Government. Raleigh: the Council, 1968.

   A survey of North Carolina's racial employment practices
   and patterns within the state's administraive
   bureaurocracy.

394.   Novak, Daniel A. The Wheel of Servitude: Black Forced Labor After Slavery. Lexington: University of Kentucky Press, 1978.

   An excellent legally oriented survey of post-Civil War
   Black Labor with analysis of Black Codes, the Freedmans
   Bureau, Reconstruction, Peonage and forced Black labor.
   Useful bibliographic notes.

395.   Novak, Daniel Allen. "Peonage: Negro Contract Labor, Sharecropping, Tenantry and the Law in the South, 1865-1970".   Diss. Brandeis, 1975.

   The author details the history and development of the legal
   system and specific laws supporting peonage. The
   difficulties of utilizing the law to dislodge peonage when
   the economic system reinforces this type of exploitation,
   are also discussed.

396.   Nyden, Paul. Black Coal Miners in the United States. New York: AIMS Press, 1974.

   Nyden looks at various components of race and class
   relations in the United Mine Workers of America (UMW).
   Racism, Black-white unity and the insurgent Minors for
   Democracy organization are given a popular and sympathetic
   treatment.
   Useful small bibliography with some primary sources listed.

397.   Offner, Paul. "Labor Force Participation in the Ghetto".   Diss. Princeton, 1970.

   The author focuses on the quantity of employment in poverty
   areas in New York city, and the relation between proximity
   of employment and employment opportunity.

398.   Ohio Historical Society.   Ohio Historical Society Archives.
Columbus: the Society, n.d.

   The Ohio Historical Society Archives Library maintains
   several manuscript collections with references to Black
   labor. The Warren Page (1911-   ) papers 1973-75 (Mss
   750) and transcripts of interviews with Black union members
   Nathaniel Lee (OHI 246) and Pauline Taylor (OHT 122,272).
   For a more detailed listing see Selected Bibliography of
   Black History Sources at the Ohio Historical Society
   (Columbus: Ohio Historical Society, 1983 by Kay Weisman)
   guide, Guide to Primary Sources in Ohio Labor History,
   (Columbus: Ohio Historical Society 1980 by Roger Meade and
   Marjorie Myers.)

399.   Olcott, Jane. Work of Colored Women. New York: National Board of
the Y.W.C.A., 1919.

   A brief look at the employment of Black women during the
   early 20th century, especially in connection with domestic
   service.

400.   Orear, Leslie and Diamond, Stephen H. Out of the Jungle.
Chicago: Hyde Park Press, 1968.

   A narrated pictorial story of the United Packinghouse, Food
   and Allied Workers, AFL-CIO since its founding in 1943.
   Numerous references to and photos of Black workers.

401.   Orr, Joesph. "The Displacement of Black High School Principals in
Selected Florida Counties and Its Relationship to Public School
Desegregation Within Them, 1967-1972".   Diss. Florida State, 1972.

   A study of the impact of desegregation upon Black high
   school principals in Florida.

402.   Ortiz, Vilma. "The Effects of Stereotypes on Rates of
Occupational Desegregation".   Diss. New York, 1981.

   The author discusses recent studies of the effect of
   stereotypical subjectivism as an explanation for varying
   rates of occupational discrimination.
   Utilizing the Bureau of Labor occupational statistics from
   1962 to 1979 for Blacks and women, the author was unable to
   substantiate a hypothesized notion of decreased
   occupational discrimination when hypothesized criteria are
   based more objectively than subjectively.

403.   Oxley, A. The Black Worker (Serials). U.S. Department of Labor
Statistics. Washington, D.C.: GPO, 1937.

404.   Ozane, Robert. The Negro in the Farm Equipment and Construction
Machinery Industry. Philadelphia: Wharton School/Industrial Research
Unit, 1972. (See Northrup, Negro Employment in Basic Industry).

405.   O'Brien, William Francis. "The Concurrent Validity of Holland's
Theory of Vocational Development Using a Sample of Non-professional Black
Workers".   Diss. Ohio State, 1975.

406.   O'Connell, Brian J. Blacks in White-collar Jobs. Montclair:
Allanheld Osmun, 1979.

        An overview of Black employment patterns in the skilled
        trades and office jobs with reference to market
        characteristics and public policy.

407.   O'Leary, Virginia Elizabeth. "The Work Acculturation of 72 Black
Women into the Labor Force: Trainee Orientation".   Diss. Wayne State,
1969.

408.   O'Neal, James. The Next Emancipation. Pamphlet No. 998.
Hampton: Hampton Institute/Peabody Collection, n.d.

409.   Paines, Herbert. Work and Retirement. Cambridge: MIT Press, n.d.

        A series of scholarly articles on retirement with sections
        devoted to Black-white labor comparisons.

410.   Painter, Nell. The Narrative of Hosea Hudson. Cambridge: Harvard
University Press, 1979.

        An oral autobiography and the most detailed personalized
        discussion of being a Black communist worker in the South
        with a focus on the period between the late 1920's and the
        Cold War period.
        The CIO, Local 2815 of the Steelworkers Union, the
        Depression and the socialization process of the Communist
        Party are explored from a perspective unique in the
        literature. Hudson's life (born in 1898, and still alive
        in 1984) illustrates a radicalization process historians
        are only recently coming to appreciate.

411.   Paradis, Adrian. Job Opportunities for Young Negroes. New York:
McKay, 1969.

        A simple "how-to" book of employment strategies for Black
        young people.

412.   Parish, Richard. Richard Parish Papers, 1950-1975. New York:
Schomburg Collection, n.d.

Richard Parish was a labor and Civil Rights activist, a the
Vice President of the United Federation of Teachers and
AFT, founder of the UFT Black caucus and coordinator of the
Negro Labor Committee.

413.   Parrow, Alan A. "Labor Sections and the Status Attainment
Process: Race and Sex Comparisons". Diss. Duke, 1981.

An empirical study utilizing National Longitudinal Surveys
of the career processes and patterns of Black and white
males and females.
The study contends that clear discrimination patterns exist
within economic sectors and sex discrimination is more
salient and dominant than racism. Micro analysis of
industries is recommended for a more detailed picture of
race and sex comparisons.

414.   Patterson, Lindsay. Anthology of the Afro-American Theatre.
Cornwell Heights: Publishers Agency, 1976.

A look at the status of Afro-Americans in the theatre
industry, with references to important events and
individuals as described by contributing authors.
(Complied under the auspices of the Association for the
Study of Afro-Amercan Life and History.)

415.   Patterson, Lindsay. Black Films and Black Filmmakers. New York:
Dodd Mead, 1975.

An overview of the film medium as relating to racial
stereotyping and a look at pictures and artists confronting
racial barriers in acting.

416.   Perlo, Victor. Economics of Racism. New York: International
Publishers, 1974.

A Marxist class analysis of recent American racial income
trends and differentials, employment discrimination,
unemployment, union and governmental influences, within the
context of a monopoly capitalist political economy. The
author also suggests a program to gain equality for
minorities.

417.   Perlo, Victor. The Negro in Southern Agriculture. New York:
International Publishers, 1953.

A detailed Marxist look at the discrimination and
exploitation experienced by Southern Black farmers and

agricultural workers in 1950.

418.   Perry, Charles R. The Negro in the Department Store Industry.
Philadelphia: Wharton School/Industrial Research Unit, 1971. (See
Northrup, Negro Employment in Basic Industry).

419.   Peterson, James. Escape from Poverty: Occupational and Economic
Mobility Among Urban Blacks. Chicago: University of Chicago/Community
and Family Study Center, 1974.

420.   Petshek, Kirk R. Negroes in the White Collar Labor Market:
Training, Employment and Attitudes. Madison: Industrial Relations
Research Institute/University of Wisconsin, 1971.

     The author attempts to understand racial employment
     barriers in the white-collar job market by comparing Black
     and white workers.
     A survey of 250 high school graduates was used, and the
     author contends that there "is little relation between
     successful employment experience" and training.

421.   Phillips, Augustus C. "Industrial Education for Negroes in the
South Atlantic Region - Development of a Program Based on Population and
Occupational Changes".   Diss. Ohio State, 1942.

422.   Phillips, William McKinley Jr. "Labor Force and Demographic
Factors Affecting the Changing Relative Status of the American Negro,
1940-1950".   Diss. University of Chicago, 1958.

423.   Pickens, William. Bursting Bonds. Boston: Jordan & More Press,
1923.

     A personalized account of the impact of slavery and its
     aftermath on the family of William Pickens who became an
     educator.

424.   Pinchbeck, Raymond. The Virginia Negro Artisan. Richmond:
William Byrd Press, 1926.

     A discussion of the condition of skilled Black workers in
     Virginia at the turn of the century.

425.   Piven, Frances and Cloward. Poor Peoples Movement. New York:
Vintage, 1979.

     The authors provide theoretical insight into the successes
     and failures of working class movements, including
     industrial workers movements, unemployment movements, the

civil and welfare rights movements. These movements have a
large percentage of Black workers and had a direct and
significant impact on Afro-Americans.

426.   Pokross, William Rodman.   "The Occupational Participation of
Younger Black Men: 'Variation Among and Recent Changes in the Larger
Metropolitan Areas'".   Diss. University of Pittsburgh, 1977.

An investigation and optimistic assessment of employment
levels of Black men, ages 20-29 working in professional,
managerial or craft positions in 26 metropolitan areas for
the years 1950, 1960 and 1970. The author suggests that
Black advances in employment reflect deeper social changes.

427.   Posner, James R.   "Income and Occupation of Negro and White
College Graduates: 1931-1966".   Diss. Princeton, 1970.

Regression analysis involving several factors (race,
father's occupation, etc.) combined with interviews of 930
Negro and white male college graduates are used to guage
results and levels of occupational success.

428.   Powers, Anne.   Blacks in American Films.   Metuchen: Scarecrow
Press, 1974.

A listing of literature on Blacks in the American film
industry.

429.   Price, Hollis F.   "The Use of Tax Incentives as a Means of
Eliminating Subemployment in the Black Community".   Diss. University of
Colorado, 1972.

A series of policy and taxation incentive proposals
"designed to induce firms to locate in center cities with
sizable Black populations".

430.   Progressive Labor Party.   A Plan for Black Liberation.   New York:
the Party, n.d.

Articles on the PLP's "Black Liberation Program", "Trade
Union Program", Constitution, Criticism and Self Criticism
and "Road to Revolution" I & II. Essentially a Maoist and
Stalinist approach to the question of the Black class
struggle in America.

431.   Pruitt, Ann S.   Black Employment in Traditionally White
Institutions in the Adams State, 1975-1977.   Atlanta: Southern
Educational Foundation, 1981.

A survey and analysis of Black employment in ten states

affected by the Adams v. Richardson employment
discrimination case between 1975 and 1977.

432.   Purcell, Theodore and Cavanagh, Gerald F.   Blacks in the
Industrial World. New York: Free Press, 1972.

A detailed look at racial attitudes and the status of the
Negro in electrical manufacturing based specifically on
field studies in Chicago, Lynchburg, Virginia, Buffalo, New
York, Memphis, Tennessee, East Pittsburgh and with a focus
on the managerial strata.

433.   Purcell, Theodore and Mulvey Daniel P.   The Negro in the
Electrical Manufacturing Industry . Philadelphia: Wharton
School/Industrial Research Unit, 1971. (See Northrup, Negro Employment
in Basic Industry).

434.   Quay, William Howard Jr.   The Negro in the Chemical Industry.
Philadelphia: Wharton School/Industrial Research Unit, 1969. (See
Northrup, Negro Employment in Basic Industry).

435.   Ramos, Maria. "A Study of Black Women in Management".   Diss.
University of Massachusetts, 1981.

Twenty Black male and female managers were asked 166
questions with measurable variables, concerning the
relation between their personal development and employment.
Chi square and qualitative analysis was used to determine
that major differences between the control groups were
insignificant. Important areas in the career development
process were identified.

436.   Randolph, A. Philip.   A. Philip Randolph and the Brotherhood
Papers. New York: A. Philip Randolph Institute, n.d.

The APRI has over 24 boxes of letters concerning the life
of A. Philip Randolph, records of the activities of the
Brotherhood of Sleeping Car Porters, the March on
Washington Movement, National Negro Congress, Negro
American Labor Council, the FEPC and other important
events. Organizations and leaders are detailed.

437.   Rattien, Stephen. "Industrial Specialization and Minority Group
Upward Mobility: A Study of Negro Employment Patterns in Selected
S.M.S.A.'s, 1950 and 1960".   Diss. Cornell, 1970.

The author attempts to identify and analyzes the process of
upward Black economic mobility, which "folows a normative
pattern".

438.   Record, Wilson. The Negro and the Communist Party. 1951; rpt.
New York: Atheneum, 1971.

The author, taking the establishment's cold-war point of
view, traces the development of the communist party's
theory and practice on the "Negro Question" in America.

439.   Register, Jasper Calvin. "Family Structure, Maternal Dominance,
Educational and Occupational Achievement: A Black-white Comparative
Analysis".   Diss. University of Kentucky, 1974.

440.   Reich, Michael. Racial Inequality: A Political Economic Analysis.
Princeton: Princeton University Press, 1981.

441.   Reid, Clifford. "Some Evidence on the Effect of Manpower Training
Programs on the Black/White Wage Differential".   Paper No. 51.
Princeton: Princeton/Industrial Relations Section, 1974.

A brief look at wage differentials between Blacks and
whites in job training programs.

442.   Reid, Ira D. and Johnson, Charles. Negro Membership in American
Labor Unions. New York: Alexander Press, 1930.

One of the best studies of the racial policies of organized
labor through the first third of the 20th century.

443.   Rexcoat, Cynthia. "Racial Differences in Wives Labor Market
Participation".   Diss. University of Illinois at Urbana-Champaign,
1980.

Utilizing national longitudinal sample data on 5000 women
ages 14 to 24, the author analyzes the effects of the labor
market structure on the participation rates of the sample
population, in connection with education levels, children
and spouse's income. The author argues that the employment
levels of married Black women is determined by the
structure of the labor market, family income maintenance
functions, metropolitan residence and specific demand for
female labor. A structural probability and recursive model
were used for factor analysis and estimates.

444.   Rhodes, Lloyd and Webb, Harvy Jr. The Book of Presidents: Leaders
of Organized Dentistry. Charlottesville: National Dental Association,
1977.

A profile of the presidents of the National Dental
Association between 1913 and 1977.

445.   Risher, Howard W. Jr.   The Negro in the Railroad Industry.
Philadelphia: Wharton School/Industrial Research Unit, 1971. (See
Northrup, Negro Employment in Basic Industry).

446.   Rittenoure, R. Lynn.   Black Employment in the South.   Austin:
University of Texas, 1976.

A look at Black employment in the federal government, with
a discussion and analysis of discriminatory employment
patterns and various policy remedies, especially in the
South.

447.   Robinson, Dorothy R.   The Bell Rings at Four.   Austin: Madrona
Press, 1978.

A non-scholarly Black teachers chronical of social change,
teaching experiences and family life in Texas.

448.   Rocha, Joseph Jr.   "The Differential Impact of an Urban Labor
Market Upon the Mobility of White and Negro Potentially Skilled Workers".
Diss. University of Iowa, 1966.

Utilizing a survey method, "...this study is focused upon a
determination, analysis and interpretation of the
differential impact of the Baltimore, Maryland labor
mobility of two selected groups of potentially skilled
workers, one white and the other Negro".

449.   Roosevelt University.   Oral History Project.   Chicago: the
University, n.d.

-Interviews with four Black female trade unionists, and a
dissident former leader of Black steel workers. The women
were interviewed as part of an interview series "20th
Century Trade Union Woman".
-Addie Wyatt-Internal Staff-Annual Meat Cutters and
Butcher Workmen of America
-Maida Springer Kemp-former staff member of Internal
Ladies Garment Workers Union
-Ola Kennedy-Local President of the United Steelworkers of
America
-Barbara Merrill-Social Workers Organization
-Rayfield Mooty-Founder of the National Committee of
Concerned Black Steelworkers Caucus Movement

450.   Ross, Arthur M. and Hill, Herbert.   Employment, Race and Poverty.
New York: Harcourt, Brace & World, 1967.

This wide ranging collection of articles focuses mainly on
the recent developments in the American economy vis-a-vis

Black workers. This work is one of the best to come out of
the 1960's literature.

451.   Rowan, Richard and Lester, Rubin. Opening the Skilled
Construction Trades to Blacks. Report No. 7. Philadelphia: Wharton
School/Industrial Research Unit, 1972.

A field survey of the impact of the Federal
Anti-discrimination policy in construction industry
employment with a specific focus on Washington, D.C., and
Indianapolis, Indiana.

452.   Rowan, Richard L. The Negro in the Textile Industry.
Philadelphia: Wharton School/Industrial Research Unit, 1970. (See
Northrup, Negro Employment in Basic Industry).

453.   Rowan, Richard L. The Negro in the Steel Industry. Philadelphia:
Wharton School/Industrial Research Unit, 1968. (See Northrup, Negro
Employment in Basic Industry).

454.   Rubin, Lester. The Negro in the Shipbuilding Industry.
Philadelphia: Wharton School/Industrial Research Unit, 1970. (See
Northrup, Negro Employment in Basic Industry).

455.   Rubin, Lester and Swift, William S. The Negro in the Longshore
Industry. Philadelphia: Wharton School/Industrial Research Unit, 1973.
(See Northrup, Negro Employment in Basic Industry).

456.   Ruchames, Louis. Race, Jobs and Politics: The Story of the FEPC.
New York: Columbia University Press, 1953.

A detailed scholarly analysis of the role of the federal
government in achieving fair employment. The New Deal, the
FEPC and several municipal employment commissions are
discussed.

457.   Rutgers University/Africana Studies Department. Afro-American
Labor Archives. New Brunswick: the University, n.d.

Founded in 1984, the AALA collects records pertaining to
Black American labor after the Civil War, Black-white labor
relations, and documentary linkages between the Labor and
Civil Rights Movements.
Among the letters, manuscripts, documents, photographs,
audio tapes, etc., are included records from the Negro
Labor Council, the Negro American Labor Committee,
Fightback (a Harlem based labor-civil rights protest
organization), the NAACP's Labor and Industrial Committee
records (NY), Brotherhood of Sleeping Car Porters' records,

and the papers of Hosea Hudson, James Haughton, Benjamine
McLaurin and Ernest Thompson are among the most important
holdings.

458.   Rutledge, Aaron L. and Grass, Gertrude Zemon. **Nineteen Negro Men.**
San Francisco: Jossey-Bass, 1967.

A psychological, non-statistical approach to the retraining
of 19 disadvantaged Afro-American men who are introduced to
practical nursing.

459.   Salmon, Jaslin U. **Black Executives in White Businesses.**   Lanham:
University Press of America, 1979.

A sympathetic, sparsely documented look at the Black
executive's struggle within the dominant corporate economic
structure.

460.   Sampson, Henry. **Blacks in Black Face.**   Metuchen: Scarecrow Press,
1980.

A discussion of early Black musical shows with photographs
of individual actors, and a discussion of conditions and
experiences of employment.

461.   Sampson, Henry T. **Blacks in Black and White: A Source Book on
Black Films.**   Metuchen: Scarecrow Press, 1977.

An annotated overview of Blacks in the film industry.

462.   Sanders, Charles L. "A Comparative Study of Black Professional
leaders: Their Perceptions of Institutional Racism and Strategies for
Dealing with Racism".   Diss. New York, 1972.

This study looks at racism in white professional
organizations, anti-racist tactics used by Black
professional groups within larger professional
organizations and implications therein.

463.   Sassen-Koob, Saskia. "Non-dominant Ethnic Populations as a
Possible Component of the United States Political Economy: The Case of
Blacks and Chicanos".   Diss. University of Notre Dame, 1974.

464.   Sauage, W. Sherman. **Blacks in the West.**   Westport: Greenwood
Press, 1976.

One of the few studies concerning the economic conditions
of Black Americans in the Western (non-slave) states. The
author explores in a detailed and scholarly manner,

principle industries, business, professionals and the Black
military experience. Politics, migration, Civil Rights and
education are also discussed thru 1890.

465.   Scarborough, D.D. Economic Study of Negro Farmers as Owners,
Tenants, and Croppers. Athens: McGregor, 1925.

One of the early studies of Afro-American farm owners and
laborers.

466.   Schermer, George. Employer's Guide to Equal Opportunity.
Washington, D.C.: Potomac Institute, 1966.

An attempt to explain EEOC anti-discrimination and equal
opportunity provisions and provide assistance to management
for the implementation of these policies.

467.   Schleiter, Mary Kay. "Occupational and Social Group: Blacks in
Internal Medicine".   Diss. University of Chicago, 1982.

A study of the process of employment differentation and
specialization among Blacks in internal medicine.
Individual and group occupational distribution was examined
and compared to other ethnic groups, as the author
concludes that social group and academic background
determine career outcome.

468.   Schomburg Collection. Blacks in the Railroad Industry Records.
New York: the Collection, n.d.

Some assorted records pertaining to the railroad
Brotherhoods.

469.   Schuster, Frederick Anthony. "An Analysis of the Effects of the
Performance of Black Males Employed as CETA Custodial Workers".   Diss.
Northern Illinois, 1979.

An analysis of employment conditions and job performance of
Black CETA custodial trainees. Regression analysis of
twelve independent variables was used to determine
regression coefficents and the larger regression equation.
The author concludes that a multiplicity of factors, many
of which are not surveyed in this study, contribute to a
CETA workers job performance.

470.   Scott, Irving J. "Professional Functions of Negro Principals in
the Public Schools of Florida".   Diss. University of Pennsylvania,
1942.

A demographic and statistical analysis of Black public

school principals in Florida.

471.   Seagrave, Charles Edwin.   "The Southern Negro Agricultural Worker:
1850-1870".   Diss. Stanford, 1971.

A quantitative, economic look at the effects of post Civil
War emancipation on conditions of Black agricultural
workers.

472.   Sethi, S. Prakash.   Business Corporations and the Black Man; An
Analysis of Social Conflict: The Kodak Fight Controversy.   San Francisco:
Chandler, 1970.

473.   Shedd, Joesph.   "White Workers and Black Trainees".   Paper No. 13.
Ithaca: Cornell University/New York School of Industrial and Labor
Relations, 1973.

An enumeration of issues and problems stemming from
training programs involving Black trainees and white
workers.

474.   Sheppard, Harold and Striner, Herbert E.   Civil Rights,
Employment and the Social Status of American Negroes.   Kalamazoo: Upjohn
Institute, 1966.

A brief look at the relationship between Civil Rights
legislation in relation to improving the conditions of
employment for Black workers.

475.   Siegel, Irving.   The Kerner Commission Report and Economic Policy.
Kalamazoo: Upjohn Institute, 1969.

A brief pamphlet focusing on the employment aspects of the
Kerner Commission Report.

476.   Simba, Malik.   "The Black Laborer, the Black Legal Experience and
the United States Supreme Court With Emphasis on the Neoconcept of Equal
Employment".   Diss. University of Minnesota, 1977.

The law, legal mechanisms, and anti-discrimination
employment cases are reviewed in connection with Supreme
Court decisions and evolving interpretation of Eual
Employment Opportunity.

477.   Simmons, Michael Eugene.   "An Inquiry into the Labor Market
Behavior of Black Youth: A Cross-sectional Analysis of the National
Longitudinal Survey Data for 1968 and 1971".   Diss. Washington State,
1979.

The author demonstrates that urban residential segregation
is a central element in the exclusion of Black youth from
the labor market. Utilizing census data comparing Black
and white youth ages 14-24, a recurcive simultaneous
equation was used to analyze national longitudinal survey
data.

478.   Simond, Ike. Old Slack's Reminiscence and Pocket History of the
Colored Profession from 1865-1981. Bowling Green: Popular Press, 1974.

A first hand account of Black minstrels, with a scholarly
preface discussing the old "colored profession".

479.   Simons, William T.   "Occupational Marginality and Social Stress: A
Comparison of Negro N.T.E. Failures and Standard Contract Teachers".
Diss. Florida State, 1966.

An empirical investigation of Southern Negro public school
teachers.

480.   Smith, James. The Convergence to Racial Equality in Women's
Wages. Santa Monica: Rand Corporation, 1978.

This brief paper explores the rise in relative wage levels
of Black women.

481.   Smith, James and Welch, Finis. Black/White Male Earnings and
Employment. Santa Monica: Rand Corporation, 1975.

A look at income differentials between 1960 and 1970,
utilizing a sample of the 1960 plus 1970 census data, and
an explanation of resulting income differences among and
between racial groups.

482.   Smith, Marvin Martin. "Essays on the Economics of Discrimination
in the Labor Market".   Diss. Cornell, 1977.

This text consists of one theoretical and one empirical
study of racial factors in the discriminatory process.
Wage differentials, wage structures and regional patterns
of discrimination are discussed.

483.   Sobin, Dennis P. The Working Poor. Port Washington: Kennikat
Press, 1973.

The author attempts to look at the social, political,
psychological, etc. impact of unemployment (low wages,
menial jobs) on Black workers. Interview, survey and
bibliographic data are used in an optimistic, idealistic
approach with an urban focus.

484.   Sovern, Michael I. Racial Discrimination in Employment.   St.
Paul: West Publishing, 1977.

This bound pamphlet, designed for courses on law and
poverty, was reprinted from a larger collection and
includes a discussion of the 1964 Civil Rights Act, Fair
Employment legislation, seniority, testing and other legal
cases concerning discriminatory employment practices.

485.   Spear, Allan H. Black Chicago: The Making of a Negro Ghetto
1890-1920. Chicago: University of Chicago Press, 1967.

This study of the development of Chicago's Black ghetto
focuses on migration, Negro leadership (deemed
accommodationist to segregationist), community segregation,
political, economic, social and institutional relations
between the majority and minority communities. Spear
weaves a social mosaic, more descriptive than analytic,
aimed at relating Negro thought to objective social
development.
The author pessimistically concludes that little progess
has been made in combating racial polorization in Chicago.
Unlike other ethnic groups, Chicago's Blacks have not
assimilated into the "melting pot".
The author's discussion of a multiplicity of sources is
good for general information on Black life in Chicago prior
to 1920. Labor references are limited, but include several
important studies on Chicago area Black labor.

486.   Spero, Sterling D. and Harris, Abram L. The Black Worker. 1931;
rpt. New York: Antheum, 1968.

The Black Worker is one of several recognized classics in
the study of Black American labor. Almost every major
study on the Black worker draws upon the work of Spero and
Harris. Black labor thru the period of the Great
Depression is discussed in connection with migration,
relations with organized labor, the economic structure of
American industry, forms of discrimination and the "Negro
middle class". The authors were not particularly
optimistic about the plight of Black workers and were
highly critical of white organized labor leadership as well
as certain Black labor leaders.
Other topics include the Black worker's heritage of
slavery, AFL craft and CIO industrial unionism, especially,
steel, coal, longshore, garment, rail and the stockyards.
Socialism and communism are also discussed in relation to a
critical estimate of the strengths and failures of party
politics vis-a-vis Black workers.
The outstanding footnotes and bibliography include economic
and racial literature, pamphlets, articles, magazines,
newspapers, federal proceedings, union records, contracts,

constitutions essential to the study of Black labor before
WWII.
As part of Columbia University's PhD thesis requirement,
Harris had chapters 2-5, 10, 14-15 and 17-19 published from
his 1931 doctorate thesis.

487.   Stanback, Howard. "Racism, Black Labor and the Giant
Corporations".   Diss. University of Massachusetts, 1980.

A case study of racism in Ford Motor Company, Jones Life
and Casualty and IBM, in which the author concludes that
overt discrimination against Black workers has declined,
but is still very strong, existing in new forms, and is
intimately tied in with the capitalist economic system.
Important statistical comparisons between Black and white
labor are made, as the author contends that Black workers
are generally worse off today, as compared with ten years
ago despite Affirmative Action.

488.   Staupers, Mabel K. No Time For Prejudice. New York: MacMillian,
1961.

One of the best treatments of Black women in the nursing
industry in the United States. The author focuses on the
organizational development of the National Association of
Colored Graduate Nurses and the process of integrating the
nursing profession. The author was also a RN and a former
president of the N.A.C.G.N.

489.   Stein, Meyer L. Blacks in Communications; Journalism, Public
Relations and Advertising. New York: Julian Messner, 1972.

490.   Stevenson, Gelvin Lee. "Determinants of the Occupational
Employment of Black and White Male Teenagers".   Diss. Washington, 1973.

A theoretical and empirical comparative study of
occupational determinants of Black and white youth
utilizing multivariate regression techniques as applied to
65 standard metropolitan areas. Statistical areas taken
from the 1960 census. Black and white youth form a dual
labor market.

491.   Stevens, George Edward. "The Personnel Decision-making Process:
An Examination of Employee Attitudes Towards Blacks and the Discernment
of Occupational Discrimination Patterns in a Simulated Environment".
Diss. Kent State, 1979.

The attitudes of 160 subjects were tested by questionaire,
in relation to racially discriminatory attitudes towards
Blacks. No linkage was found between attitudes and
behavior of the interviewees towards Blacks in a

hypothetical employment condition.

492.   Stokes, Allen Heath Jr.   "Black and White Labor and the
Development of the Southern Textile Industry, 1800-1920".   Diss.
University of South Carolina, 1977.

A detailed study of the transition of the Southern textile
labor force and the replacement of Black with white labor
in the mills after the Civil War. The perpetuation of
racism by textile industrialists is viewed as a key element
in southern social relations. During the WWI period, labor
shortages forced industrialists to employ more Blacks in
South Carolina, and get rid of them after the war.

493.   Stolzenberg, Mark.   "Occupational Differences in Wage
Discrimination Against Black Men: The Struggle of Racial Differences in
Men's Wage Returns to Schooling, 1960".   Diss. University of Michigan,
1973.

This study attempts to measure "the extent to which Black
men recieve a lower wage return on their educational
investments than white men in the same occupation..."

494.   Strauss, Robert P.   "Discrimination Against Negroes in the Labor
Market: The Impact of Market Structure on Negro Employment".   Diss.
Madison Wisconsin, 1970.

The author measures and discusses job discrimination
against Afro-Americans, economic status, skills, income and
poverty trends are explored.

495.   Street, James H.   The Revolution in the Cotton Economy.   Chapel
Hill: University of Carolina Press, 1957.

A detailed discussion of the mechanization if the cotton
industry with numerous references to Black agricultural
workers including sharecroppers and tenant farmers.
Outstanding bibliography on the topic of
cotton/agricultural mechanization.

496.   Swain, Johnnie Dee Jr.   "Regional Comparison of Black and White
Women Economic Activities in Segmented Labor markets: Implication for
Social Policy".   Diss. Syracuse, 1977.

An explanation of racial differences in the labor force
participation patterns of Black and white married urban
females. Multiple regression analysis, census data and
other quanitative techniques highlight the differences in
labor force participation patterns of the two groups of
women.

497.   Swan, James.   "Racism in Labor Markets".   Vols. I, II.   Diss.
Northwestern, 1981.

An attempt to integrate Marxist analysis of capitalism with
Marxist analysis of racism in the context of capitatalist
labor markets, contradictions within the working class, and
contradictions between individual and capitalist class
necessities in order to explain racism in the labor market.
Utilizing census data, and other statistical sources,
unionization, wages, unemployment, etc., this study finds
no evidence linking white worker gains with racial
inequality.
The author suggests that no single theory satifactorily
explains racism in the market place, and outlines a
direction for future theoretical development.

498.   Sweet, James A.   Women in the Labor Force.   New York: Seminar
Press, 1973.

One of the best "main stream" statistical and analytical
approaches, albeit highly focused on the labor force
activity of wives, including Blacks, in the context of
categorical influences and comparisons pertaining to
employment.

499.   Swift, William S.   The Negro in the Offshore Maritime Industry.
Philadelphia: Wharton School/Industrial Research Unit, 1973.   (See
Northrup, Negro Employment in Basic Industry).

500.   Theiblot, Armand J. Jr.   The Negro in the Banking Industry.
Philadelphia: Wharton School/Industrial Research Unit, 1970.   (See
Northrup, Negro Employment in Basic Industry).

501.   The Civil Rights Congress.   The Civil Rights Congress Record
Group.   New York: Schomburg Collection, n.d.

An out growth of the International Labor Defense Fund
(founded in 1927) to help oppressed workers, the Congress
was deeply involved in labor and Civil Rights activity. By
the 1950's the Congress was influential, nationally known
and recognized around the world. The Congress, led by
William Patterson, was a victim of the 1950's cold war and
stopped functioning in 1955.

502.   The Committee on Fair Employment.   Records of the Committee
on Fair Employment, 1941-1946.   New York: Microfilm Corporation, 1946.

The FEPC was established by President Frankiln D. Roosevelt
in 1941 in an effort to avoid a massive civil rights march
sponsored by A Philip Randolph. Thousands of documents

including field reports, correspondence, case records, thousands of discrimination complaints and data relating to defense, union membership, employment conditions, etc., are located in the National Archives, and are available in microfilm collections.

503.   The Negro Publication Society of America. "The South Moves West". The Negro Quarterly. Vol. II. Nos. 1, 2. New York: the Society, 1944.

This two part special edition deals with the question of discrimination in the boilermakers union and issues of a more general nature confronting Black workers as addressed by a few contributors (Angelo Herndon, editor).

504.   Thompson, Cleopatra. The History of the Mississippi Teachers Association. Jackson: Mississippi Teachers Association, 1973.

A review of the role of Black teachers played in the Mississippi public school system.

505.   Thompson, Mindy. "The National Negro Labor Council: A History". Occupational Paper No. 27. New York: AIMS Press, 1978.

This document is an outline history, based on original sources and documents of the NNLC. The NNLC, as an expression and outgrowth of the proletarianization of the Black working class, is traced from its founding convention in Chicago (1929) to its disbanding in 1956 because of intense red baiting and federal harassment. The Subversive Activity Control Board (SCAB) declared NNLC subversive. Afro-American communists were among its leaders. The NNLC was very influential in the CIO's industrial organizing campaigns among Black workers. Its early founders and supporters included Coleman Young, Paul Robeson and Harry Belefonte. The vacuum created by the NNLC's demise was in part, filled by the emergence of the coalition of Black Trade Unionists. Also containing a good brief bibliography for original source material.

506.   Traillion, Joesph T. Jr. "A Study of the Characteristics and Career Patterns of White and Non-white Elementary Principals in Four Urban School Systems". Diss. University of Colorado, 1973.

A study of the career patterns of Black and white principals based on a survey of 209 educators in Atlanta, Denver, Jackson (Mississippi) and Rockford (Illinois).

507.   Transport Workers Union of America-AFL-CIO. TWU and the Flight for Civil Rights. New York: the Union, 1963.

A pamphlet discussion of the relationship between the
Transport Workers Union and the Civil Rights Movement
between 1934-1963.

508.   Trigg, Martelle D.   "Differential Mobility Among Black and White
Physicians in the State of Tennessee".   Diss. University of Tennessee,
1972.

Based upon a survey of 848 physicians, this thesis attempts
to determine the social, economic and demographic factors
contributing to job mobility among Black and white doctors
in Tennessee.

509.   Troy, Leo.   Organized Labor in New Jersey.   Princeton: D. Van
Nostrand, 1965.

This volume of New Jersey history traces the development of
local organized labor, and contains important references to
the relationship of Black labor and trade unionism.

510.   Turgeon, Lynn.   The Economics of Discrimination.   Budapest:
Hungarian Academy of Sciences/Center for Afro-Asian Research, 1973.

A brief discussion of some of the major theoretical
approaches to the question of economic discrimination.

511.   Turner, Ralph.   "Some Factors in the Differential Position of
Whites and Negroes in the Labor Force of the United States".   Diss.
University of Chicago, 1949.

An analysis of social and economic factors tending to
create or reinforce employment discrimination against Black
workers focusing on the WWII period.

512.   Tyson, Roberta Shade.   "A Descriptive Study of Factors Influencing
the Professional Mobility of Black Female Administrators in Public
Education in Louisiana Between 1952 and 1978".   Diss. George Peabody,
1980.

A look at educational experiences, political affiliations,
family backgroud, etc., in relation to the upward mobility
of Black female administrators employed in Louisiana's
public school system between 1952 and 1978. The author
stresses the importance of education, political
affiliations, race and sex, in that order, as mobility
factors.

513.   University of Connecticut/Labor Education Center.   Blacks in the
Building Trades Labor Education.   Storrs: the University,   1970.

A policy oriented study of Black participation in the
building trades in Connecticut including a discussion of
unions, employers, and apprenticeship programs.

514.   University of Missouri. <u>Western Historical Manuscript Collection</u>
<u>and the State Historical Society of Missouri Manuscripts.</u> Columbia: the
University, n.d.

Collections containing information on black labor in
specialized occupational categories include the St. Louis
Typographical Union Collection; references to Black
teachers in collection 2891 North Central Association of
Colleges and Secondary Schools, Papers, 1932-1965;
collection 3551 U.S. Work Projects Administration,
Historical Records Survey, Missouri; and collection 2220
Forrest Smith Papers, 1853-1945 has three index references
to black laborers. The Black Municipal Labor Coalition,
St. Louis is mentioned in collection 3634 Carpenters Joint
Apprenticeship Committee, St. Louis, Missouri, Records,
1964-1981.

Some of the territorial collections have references to the
hiring of Blacks and Black laborers. Other collections
concerning Black labor in general are:

1036- William Clark Breckenridge Papers (reference to
Black laborers in the 1870's)
1082- Social and Economic Census of the Colored
Population, 1901, Columbia, Missouri
3131- Frank Ely Atwood Papers, 1888-1943 (one reference to
Blacks and labor unions in the 1930's)
3187- University of Missouri, Agricultural Assistance
Programs, records, 1951-1966 (one reference to Black
laborers)
3475- Missouri Association for Social Welfare Papers (two
references to Blacks and unemployment in the 1950's)
This collection is restricted and permission for use
and/or copying must be obtained from the Executive
Secretary, President, or other officer of the MASW, 412
Jefferson Street, Jefferson City, Missouri 65101.

515.   Urban League of Kansas City. <u>The Negro Worker of Kansas City.</u>
Kansas City: the League, n.d.

A study of trade union and organized labor relations in
1939-1940, as prepared by the Department of Industrial
Relations of the Urban League of Kansas City.

516.   U.S. Bureau of Labor Statistics. <u>Directory of Data Sources on</u>
<u>Racial and Ethnic Minorities.</u> Washington, D.C.: GPO, 1975.

A useful guide to government data on Blacks and other

minorities citing sources of economic data.

517. U.S. Bureau of the Census. Distribution of Occupational Employment in the States by Race and Sex. Washington, D.C.: GPO, 1980.

518. U.S. Bureau of the Census. Negroes in the United States (1910). Washington, D.C.: GPO, 1915.

    Contains good urban occupational and rural agricultural information, especially for the Black Belt.

519. U.S. Bureau of the Census. The Social and Economic Status of the Black Population in the United States: An Historic View, 1790-1978. Washington, D.C.: GPO, 1979.

    An overview of the socioeconomic progress of Black Americans comparing many decades of census data and indicating long term trends.

520. U.S. Commission on Civil Rights. A Sharper Look at Unemployment in the U.S. Cities. Washington, D.C.: GPO, 1964.

    This volume is a summary report submitted to the President and evaluates programs, problems and policies vis-a-vis urban unemployment, of which a large percentage is Black.

521. U.S. Commission on Civil Rights. Federal Civil Rights Enforcement Effort. Washington, D.C.: GPO, 1970.

    An evaluation of various federal agencies and their attempts to implement Civil Rights laws focusing on the year 1970. Much of the emphasis of this document is on employment and civil rights policies, litigation and perscription to improve the enforcement mechanism.

522. U.S. Commission on Civil Rights. Last Hired, First Fired: Layoffs and Civil Rights. Washington, D.C.: GPO, 1977.

    A study of the impact of layoff procedures upon women and minorities.

523. U.S. Commission on Civil Rights. Nonreferral Unions and Equal Employment Opportunity. Washington, D.C.: GPO, 1972.

    A report on production, maintenance and service workers in 12 large unions including the auto, steel, and electrical workers unions, focusing on worksite situations and policies affecting minority and female job advancement. A good dicussion and statistical information on Black union leadership is also presented.

524.   U.S. Commission on Civil Rights. Social Industries of Equality
for Minorities and Women. Washington, D.C.: GPO, 1978.

A survey of industries providing access and upward mobility
for Blacks and women.

525.   U.S. Commission on Civil Rights. The Challenge Ahead: Equal
Opportunity in Referral Unions. Washington, D.C.: GPO, 1976.

A study of minority and female employment opportunities in
unions that directly control or influence entry into a
trade, especially in relation to apprenticeship as most
often occurs in the skilled trade and crafts unions.

526.   U.S. Commission on Civil Rights. U.S. Commission on Civil Rights
Equal Employment under the Federal Law. Report No. 5. Washington, D.C.:
GPO, 1966.

A review of equal employment policies and practices
conducted during the height of the modern Civil Rights
Movement.

527.   U.S. Congressional Budget Office. Income Disparities Between
Black and White Americans. Washington, D.C.: GPO, 1977.

A useful review of Black, white wage differentials, factors
contributing to income disparities and federal policies
affecting racial income.

528.   U.S. Congress. House Joint Economic Committee. Minority
Employment Opportunities, 1980-1985: Hearings. 96th Congress, first
session. Washington, D.C.: GPO, 1980.

Testimony of a broad range of people concerning minority,
especially Black, employment opportunity.

529.   U.S. Congress. National Commission of Manpower Policy. The
Economic Position of Black Americans. Washington, D.C.: GPO, 1976.

A study of the economic status of Black Americans in 1975,
revealing the second class position held in the economy by
Afro-Americans.

530.   U.S. Department of Labor. Division of Negro Economics. Negro
Migration in 1916-17. Reports by R.H. Leavell et al. 1919; rpt.
Westport: Negro Universities Press, 1969.

This publication focuses on the economic aspects of early 20th century Black migration from the South to the North.

531.   U.S. Department of Labor. Division of Negro Economy. The Negro at Work During the World War and During Reconstruction. 1921; rpt. New York: Negro Universities Press, 1969.

A statistical and analytical study of Black employment in basic industries desegregated because of the war induced labor shortages. Reports from eleven states are included with illustrations and tables revealing dramatic increases in Black industrial employment.

532.   U.S. Women's Bureau. Negro Women in Industry. Washington, D.C.: GPO, 1922.

An overview of Black female participation in industrial employment during the early 20th century.

533.   Vines, Dwight D. "The Impact of Title VII of the 1964 Civil Rights Law on Personnel Policies and Practices." Diss. University of Colorado, 1967.

Interviews were conducted with managers in 20 sample firms in one northern and one southern city to contrast the impact of the 1964 Civil Rights law on employment practices in the targeted industries. The author cited contradictions, inconsistencies and limitations in the application of Title VII, while recognizing positive change, especially in the South.

534.   Wachel, Dawn. The Negro and Discrimination in Employment. Detroit: University of Michigan/Wayne State, 1965.

This monograph discusses some of the literature pertaining to Black employment discrimination in relation to major barriers confronting Black advancement.

535.   Walker, James L. Economic Development and Black Employment in the Nonmetropolitan South. Austin: University of Texas/Bureau of Business Research, 1977.

The author looks at the factors statistically influencing Black rural non-farm employment participation and contends that education is the key to economic development in the face of racial discrimination.

536.   Walker, Wilda Renee. "A Study of Black Consciousness as a Model for Examining the Relationship Between Self-perceived Status and Ethnocentricism in Black Social Workers". Diss. Howard, 1980.

537.   Wallace, Phyllis A.   Black Women in the Labor Force.   Cambridge:
MIT Press, 1980.

This is one of the few, and one of the best books on Black
women workers in the United States.   Utilizing census data
and various studies, the author statistically demonstrates
the exploited position of Black women in the labor force.
Wages, occupational development categories, shifts in the
employment characteristics and discrimination against Black
women are analyzed in relation to other ethnic labor force
participants.   A valuable critical evaluation of current
major economic literature is presented in connection with
the education, marriage, age, children and market position
of Black female workers.   Policy and research suggestions
are made in conclusion.
The footnotes and bibliography based mainly on articles and
census data are outstanding resources for economic
literature on the Black woman.

538.   Wallace, Phyllis and LaMond, Annette M.   Women, Minorities and
Employment Discrimination.   Lexington: Lexington Books, n.d.

A collection of scholarly articles focusing on theories of
economic discrimination, worker expectation in relation to
discriminatoin, the psychology of female labor force
participation, Black employment in the South, segmented
labor markets, racial income differentials and recommended
areas of further research.

539.   Wallace, Phyllis A., ed.   Equal Employment Opportunity and the AT
and T Case.   Cambridge: MIT Press, 1976.

A detailed collection of articles focusing on employment
discrimination in the American Telephone and Telegraph
Company.   A theory of discrimination is presented, and
other economic facets of employment discrimination are
covered including wage differentials, the cost of
discrimination, occupational segregation, equality in the
work place, gender variables, management's role in racial
discrimination and the impact of federal laws and
institutions on pervuasive patterns of job related
discrimination.

540.   Walsh, Edward J.   Job Stigma and Self Esteem.   Ann Arbor:
University of Michigan, 1974.

A participant/observation study of garbage men and
Municipal workers (many of whom are Black) concerning their
job perceptions and self esteem.

541.   Walters, Raymond. Negroes and the Great Depression. Westport:
Greenwood Press, 1970.

An examination of the agricultural, and industrial
conditions of, and governmental New Deal programs for
Negroes in the Depression period. Black political
influence upon the New Deal and the NAACP's role during the
economic crisis are also detailed.

542.   Wandner, Stephen A. "Racial Patterns of Employment in
Indianapolis: The Implications for Fair Employment Practices Policy".
Diss. University of Indiana, 1972.

A detailed description of the economic aspects of
employment discrimination against Black men in the
Indianapolis statistical metropolitan area.

543.   Warren, Samuel Enders. "The Negro in the American Labor
Movement".   Diss. University of Wisconsin, 1942.

A highly detailed sympathetic study of economic, political
and social forces shaping the participation of Blacks in
the Trade Union Movement. One of the best dissertations
from the pre-WWII period concerning Blacks and labor.

544.   Washington, Philemon. "The Job Satisfaction of Black Public
School Administrators in New Jersey".   Diss. University of Minnesota,
1974.

This study is based on a survey of 282 Black
administrators- compared to 150 white administrators,
showing whites more satisfied with their jobs than Blacks.

545.   Watkins, Don and McKinney, David. A Study of Employment Patterns
in the General Merchandise Group Retail Stores in New York City. New
York City. Commission of Human Rights. New York: the Commission, 1966.

An attempt to gauge equal employment progress, problems and
prospects as reported by major retail executives, and based
on work force distribution data.

546.   Weaver, Robert C. Negro Labor a National Problem. Port
Washington: Kennikat Press, 1946.

Based mainly on material drawn from periodicals, this text
examines barriers to Black employment, wartime employment,
transportation, seniority, full employment, management,
government and union-Black relationships.

547.   Weaver, Robert Clifton. Robert Clifton Weaver Papers; 1869,

<u>1923-70</u>. New York: Schomburg Collection, n.d.

    Robert Weaver was the first Black presidential cabinet
officer (HUD-LBJ, Housing and Urban Development under
President Johnson), a trained economist, Harvard graduate
and noted scholar on Black labor.

548.   Weiner, Stuart E. "A Survival Analysis of Adult Black/White
Unemployment Rate Differentials".   Diss. Northwestern, 1982.

    A comparison of Black/white employment, unemployment and
nonparticipation in the labor force, drawn from the Denver
and Seattle income mainetance experiments, seeking to
explain employment rate differences. Race is viewed as the
main factor (as opposed to class, education, personal
skills, experience, etc.) in understanding the Black
unemployment rate differentials which are generally twice
as great as the rate for

549.   Weiss, Randall D. "The Effects of Education on the Earnings of
Blacks and Whites". Paper No. 44. Cambridge: Harvard/Program on
Regional and Urban Economics, 1969.

    The author demonstrates that education is not the major
determinant of the income levels for Blacks.

550.   Wells, John C. "Teacher Militancy and Professional Orientation
Amongst Black Teachers in New York State".   Diss. New York, 1976.

    An interesting story of Black teachers linking client
orientation to militancy.

551.   Wesley, Charles. <u>Negro Labor in the United States: 1850-1925</u>.
1927; rpt. New York: Russell & Russell, 1967.

    A sympathetic, scholarly and classic study of the first
large scale industrialization process experienced by Black
workers between 1850 and 1925. Valuable references for
detailed information on that period are included.

552.   Wesson, William Hinton. <u>Negro Employment Practices in the</u>
<u>Chattanooga Area</u>. Committee of the South. Selected Studies of Negro
Employment in the South. Case Study No. 5. Washington, D.C.: National
Planning Association, 1954.

    A look at racial employment barriers and patterns in
Chattanooga during the early 1950's.

553.   Whaley, George Leeandrew. "The Impact of Title VII of the 1964
Civil Rights Act Upon Contract Provisions Regarding Seniority Systems and

Black Employment Within the Atomic Energy Industry".   Diss. University
of Colorado at Boulder, 1974.

A statistically-oriented survey of Title VII's impact on
the perceptions, practices and policies of labor and
management in relation to Black men and the atomic energy
industry.

554.   Whitted, Christine. "Supports in the Black Community: Black
Unmarried Mothers who kept their Babies and Achieved their Educational
and/or Professional Goals".   Diss. Columbia, 1978.

Informal interviews and analysis of 10 case studies and
community support systems for Black mothers.

555.   Wiggins, Elnora. "An Analysis of the Teaching Strengths and
Weaknesses of Black Business Teachers in the Southeastern United States".
Diss. University of Mississippi, 1975.

A look at the skills level of Black high school business
teachers based on a survey/evaluation of administrators and
teachers.

556.   Williams, Bruce Burnette. "Black Suburbanization and Dual Labor
Market Theory: An Empirical Study".   Diss. University of Chicago, 1979.

A detailed study of the employment/umemployment of Black
youth ages 18-30, in relation to labor market entry and
advancement in a suburban Chicago light production
industry. Utilizing an open ended questionaire of
management and labor, the author details a specific
constellation of discrimination which is unexplained by
traditional economic or dual market theory.

557.   Williams, Carolyn R. Armstrong. "Education for Black
Participation in the Labor Movement: A Case Study".   Diss. Cornell,
1978.

A look at discrimination in a Philadelphia International
Brotherhood of Electrical Workers Local.

558.   Williams, Edward. The First Black Captain. New York: Vantage,
1974.

An autobiography of Newark, New Jersey's first Black police
captain- Edward Williams.

559.   Williams, Walter E. The State Against Blacks. Manhattan
Institute for Policy Research Books. New York: New Press, 1982.

A neoconservative view of racial discrimination stressing
non-racial factors in explaining the inferior economic
status of Black Americans. The author cites economic
advances of Southeast Asians as evidence of nonracial
factors accounting for progress. The minimum wage is
attacked, as are regulations and unions in taxi, railroad,
trucking and skilled trade industries. The author
advocates a "free market" approach, and is opposed to
federal economic intervention on behalf of minorities.

560. Wilson Library. The Southern History Collection. Chapel Hill:
University of North Carolina, n.d.

This collection contains some taped interviews with Black
tobacco workers.

561. Wilson, Joan. "The Emergence and Development of a Black
Intervention Organization: JAP". Diss. New York, 1977.

A discussion of the emergence, in 1964, of the Joint
Apprenticeship Program connected with the A.P. Randolph
Institute.

562. Wilson, Joesph. Documentary Video Interview Series of
Afro-American Labor Leaders. New York: Schomburg Collection, 1984.

-Lillian Roberts- New York State Labor Commission
-Hosea Hudson- Steelworker, radical
-Benjamin McLaurin- East Coast Zone Supervisor of the
Brotherhood of Sleeping Car Porters
-Cleveland Robinson- Secretary Treasurer District 65, New
York Distributive Workers of America
-Doris Turner- President 1199 Hospital Workers Union
-Addie Wyatt- Vice President, Food and Commercial Workers
-Bill Lucy- Secretary Treasurer A.F.S.C.M.E.

This video series examines family histories, community and
civil rights linkages, labor and union experiences of
important Black labor leaders. Produced by James Murry,
Director of the Audio Visual Department at the Schomburg
Library.

563. Wilson, Joseph. "Cold Steel: The Political Economy of Black Labor
and Reform in the United States". Diss. Columbia, 1980.

A field study and analysis of the 1977 Reform Movement in
the steelworkers union, focusing on the role of Black
workers in the Steelworkers Fight Back electorial campaign.
Black workers tended to play a militant role in the
movement, and identified racially in Black caucuses, and
with the larger class of workers seeking Democratic rank
and file oriented reform. Based upon interviews, and

working in the election process itself, the author presents
a unique view of the interaction between union and racial
politics, in the context of a monopoly dominated
capitalistic political and economic system.

564.   Witt, Tom S.   "The Regional Racial Unemployment Rate".   Diss.
Washington, 1974.

An attempt to explain the magnitude of 'racial/regional'
unemployment in the United States. A useful review of the
literature on unemployment contained in second chapter.

565.   Wofford, Benjamin Monroe and Kelly, T.A.   Mississippi Workers:
Where They Come From and How They Perform.   University: University of
Alabama Press, 1955.

A study of the employment demographics of 3 Mississippi
factories during the post WWII period.

566.   Wolfe, French Eugene.   Admission to American Trade Unions.
Baltimore: John Hopkins University Press, 1912.

An outstanding, scholarly historic development of the
racial policies of American trade unions during the early
1900's that excluded Black membership and limited Black
employment.

567.   Wolkinson, Benjamine W.   Blacks, Unions and The EEOC.   Lexington:
Lexington Books, 1973.

One of the best discussions of recent union discrimination
practices (75 case studies) and the role of the Equal
Employment Opportunities Commission as a vehicle of
conciliation. Useful bibliograhy of relevant government
publications, legal cases and union documents.

568.   Wonderlic, E.F.   Negro Norms.   Northfield: E.F. Wonderlic and
Associates, n.d.

This is a statistical study of 38,452 job applicants for
affirmative action programs. Methods of data collection,
standards and usage are included with the Wonderlic
personnel text.

569.   Woodson, Carter.   The Negro Professional Man and the Community.
1934; rpt. New York: Negro Universities Press, 1969.

570.   Woodson, Carter G.   The Mis-education of the Negro.   Washington,
D.C.: Associated Publishers, 1969.

This classic study treats educational questions pertaining
to Black people as sociological, vocational and
professional in character. Education plays a central role
in tha application of social labor, social institutions and
racial values determine the content, nature and orientation
of vocational/professional training in a pervasive
discriminatory environment.

571.   Woodson, Carter G.   The Rural Negro.   New York: Russell & Russell,
1930.

An outstanding indepth study of the southern rural
conditions of labor among Black workers betwen 1875 and
1930, including tenancy, peonage, industry and trade.

572.   Woodward, Maurice C.   Blacks and Political Science.   Washington,
D.C.: APSA, 1977.

A survey of the status, curriculum and attitudes of Black
political scientists.

573.   Woofter, T. J. Jr.   Black Yeomanry.   New York: Henry Holt, 1930.

A description of life in the Island of St. Helena with
reference to agricultural and farm labor within this unique
Afro-American Community.

574.   Works Progress Administration.   The Negro in New York.   New York:
the Administration, 1940.

A detailed discussion of the economic status of Blacks in
New York with reference to employment, trade unionism and
the Harlem boycott movement focused on the 125th Street
employment discrimination.

575.   Work, John.   Race, Economics and Corporate America.   Wilmington:
Scholarly Resources, 1984.

An analysis of racial discrimination and employment,
especially within the corporate context. Income, mobility,
labor market dynamics, hiring, training, etc. are discussed
in relation to theoretical considerations given to the
process of economic discrimination.
Corporate personnel data are analysized in relation to the
status of Black employees as the author suggests policies
for equal opportunity within these modern economic
entities.

576.   Work in America: Report of a Special Task Force to the Secretary

of Health, Education, and Welfare. Cambridge: MIT Press, 1973.

577.   Wright, Carroll D. The Industrial Progress of the South.
Hampton: Hampton Institute/Peabody Collection, n.d.

578.   Wright, Richard Robert Jr. A Study of the Industrial Conditions
of the Negro Population of Pennsylvania and Especially the Cities of
Philadelphia and Pittsburgh. Harrisburg: Pennsylvania Bureau of
Industrial Statistics, 1914.

     A highly detailed report concerning Black urban industrial
     workers in 3 cities, and their limited access to employment
     at the turn of the century.

579.   Wrong, Elaine Gale. The Negro in the Apparel Industry.
Philadelphia: Wharton School/Industrial Research Unit, 1973. (See
Northrup, Negro Employment in Basic Industry).

580.   W.P.A. Writer's Project. These are Our Lives. Salem: Ayer, 1939.

     Included are a number of interviews with Black workers
     during the Depression era.

581.   Young, Herman. "An Educated and Professional Profile of Black
American Doctorates in the Natural Sciences".   Diss. Indiana, 1973.

     A look at Black scientists and the role of education in
     career choices.

582.   Young, Herman and Barbara. Scientists in the Black Perspective.
Lexington: Lincoln Foundation, 1974.

     A discussion of important Black scientists, and a look at
     discrimination in the field of scientific employment.

583.   Zion, Carol. "The Desegregation of a Public Junior College: A
Case Study of Its Negro Faculty".   Diss. Florida State, 1964.

     This study looks at the effect of administrative decisions
     on Negro faculty.

TITLE INDEX

526

Dissertations/Papers:

SUBJECT INDEX

About the Editor

JOSEPH WILSON is Assistant Professor in the African Studies Department at Rutgers University. He received a grant from the Ford Foundation for his work on the Afro-American Archives at Rutgers. He has contributed articles to *Oral History Review* and *African Urban Quarterly*.